DOUBLETALK

50
Comedy Duets
for Actors

by
BILL
MAJESKI

MERIWETHER PUBLISHING LTD
Colorado Springs, Colorado

Meriwether Publishing Ltd., Publisher
P.O. Box 7710
Colorado Springs, CO 80933

Book Design: Tom Myers
Photography: Ted Zapel
Executive Editor: Arthur L. Zapel
Typography: Sharon E. Garlock

© Copyright MCMXC Meriwether Publishing Ltd.
Printed in the United States of America
First Edition

Library of Congress Cataloging-in-Publication Data

Majeski, Bill.
    Doubletalk : 50 comedy duets for actors / by Bill Majeski.
        p.   cm.
    ISBN 0-916260-66-6
    1. Dialogues.   2. Comedy.   I. Title.
    PN4291.M47   1990
    812'.54--dc20
                                       90-52981
                                          CIP

TABLE OF CONTENTS

TWO MEN

TWO WOMEN

OPTIONAL

NOTE: The numerals running vertically down the left margin of each page of dialog are for the convenience of the director. With these, he/she may easily direct attention to a specific passage.

INTRODUCTION

Comedy teams have been a vital part of the history of American humor. From Laurel and Hardy in films, to the earliest days of Weber and Fields, along with Smith and Dale in burlesque and vaudeville, comedy duos have brought laughter to millions of American and world-wide audiences.

Later, Dean Martin and Jerry Lewis, Rowan and Martin on Laugh-in and the Smothers Brothers were familiar figures in television two-man teams. Usually they played bright guy against the dopey partner. The conflicting personalities made the writing of the scripts a bit easier for those who provided the comedy material.

George Burns and Gracie Allen were the first big stars doing stand-up in the male/female category. Along came Mike Nichols and Elaine May, followed by Jerry Stiller and Anne Meara to brighten up our television screens. The character difference between man and woman provides instant conflict, a basic ingredient in comedy.

The success of comedy duos of two women has been less notable. Frankly, I can't think of any two-female teams that have made it big, although I'm sure that there have been some.

But don't let that stop you ladies. Perhaps you can master some of the enclosed sketches and be the first kids on the block to move up the comedy ladder.

So, ladies, take a shot at it. You'll have plenty of people pulling for you. I know I will. Good luck to all you performers, and always leave them laughing.

MEN AND WOMEN

New Addition to the Sports Staff?

CAST: ANNOUNCER, male or female. Can be Off-Stage. FRANK EDGEWORTH, sports editor of the Daily Quotidian; NANCY ANDREWS, sportswriter/job applicant.

SETTING: Sports department of the newspaper. Desk and a chair or two are only props needed.

AT RISE: FRANK EDGEWORTH, sleeves rolled up, is going over some copy at the desk. ANNOUNCER comes in to address the audience. (Or he/she can make the opening statement from Off-Stage.)

ANNOUNCER: One of the more noticeable changes in the field of journalism these days is the increase of women on newspapers' editorial staffs. This is particularly true of young ladies working in the sports field.

Oh, there has been some controversy about this, but it hasn't stopped eager, talented young women from gaining a foothold in this previously all-male domain.

Ah, here comes another aspiring sportswriter looking for employment. *(ANNOUNCER leaves. NANCY ANDREWS enters bouncily, smiling and eager. EDGEWORTH gestures her to sit down and she does.)*

EDGEWORTH: *(Glancing at paper in front of him)* **Nancy Andrews?**

NANCY: Right.

EDGEWORTH: So you want a job with us, Miss Andrews?

NANCY: Yes sir. *(Falling into sports page jargon now)* **I'd like to nab a post as sports scribe.**

EDGEWORTH: What sports can you write?

NANCY: *(Enthusiastically)* **The diamond game, gridiron sport, court action, rink roughhousing, covering thin-clad**

1 harriers as they traverse the countryside, *(She gets up and*
2 *jogs around the desk)* **track and field.** *(Here she clears an*
3 *imaginary hurdle and then sits down.)* **Any sport at all.**
4 **EDGEWORTH:** We'll be needing a baseball writer soon.
5 **NANCY:** That's my main game. There's nothing I'd rather do
6   than describe how a rubber-armed right-hander
7   outclasses a sneaky-fast southpaw in nine thrill-packed
8   stanzas of scoreless twirling, piling up goose eggs on the
9   board until Big Bart Genson comes through with a circuit
10   clout *(Stands up and takes power swing)* when all the
11   marbles were down to cop the tilt for the perennial
12   favorites. *(Sits down.)*
13 **EDGEWORTH:** Sounds pretty good.
14 **NANCY:** I also like to write stunning comeback stories where
15   the cellar dwellers keep the awestruck stands in popeyed
16   amazement by surging from behind with a last-ditch rally
17   after a titanic struggle.
18 **EDGEWORTH:** Those ball games are pretty easy to handle.
19   How do you do routs, games that end in a seventeen-two
20   score?
21 **NANCY:** Oh, you're talking about those moral victories that
22   are always closer than the final score indicates.
23 **EDGEWORTH:** Exactly.
24 **NANCY:** Those games usually happen when the Badgers, a
25   team of destiny, invade Muskrat Field to take on the lowly
26   Bruins, who are weak but willing, down, but not out. The
27   Bruins, of course, will have to throw caution to the wind
28   if they are to stop their losing skein. They end up
29   outscored, but not outfought.
30 **EDGEWORTH:** You seem well versed on the game itself.
31   What about the players? The catcher — what does he do?
32 **NANCY:** The scrappy backstop handles the deliveries of
33   flame-throwing lefties and raw-boned right-handers. *(She*
34   *suits action to her words by throwing first lefty, then righty. Sits*
35   *down.)*

1   EDGEWORTH: And the infield?
2   NANCY: There we have the initial sack keeper, hustling
3   second-sacker, peppy shortstop and a stocky hot-corner
4   guardian who won't let any scorching grounder get
5   through.
6   EDGEWORTH: And the outfield?
7   NANCY: Patrolling the outer pastures we find the lumbering
8   left fielder, *(Stands and lumbers a few steps)* the fleet center
9   gardener, *(Speeds up briefly)* and the strong-armed farm
10   boy in right. *(Throws hard and then sits down.)*
11 EDGEWORTH: And how about the front office?
12 NANCY: Well, any successful unit needs a good brain trust to
13   make John Q. Public continue to make those turnstiles
14   click. You have to have shrewd high brass who can make
15   vital acquisitions and fill the roster with hurlers who can
16   fling that pellet, *(Stands and flings that pellet)* ball hawks
17   who can really go get 'em, *(She does so and then sits)* and a
18   band of doughty warriors who never give up, no matter
19   what the score.
20 EDGEWORTH: Think you could handle spring training?
21 NANCY: The Citrus Circuit? Grapefruit League stories are
22   my meat and drink. There we have the *(Creaky voice)*
23   *a-a-a-g*ing veteran, the new *phee*nom, the shortstop with
24   two good years left and spring hitters who will be sent
25   home when the pitchers start throwing curves.
26 EDGEWORTH: And when the players sign contracts?
27 NANCY: In the steaming Southern sun the players usually
28   join the fold by inking a pact calling for salary terms that
29   are mutually agreeable.
30 EDGEWORTH: You seem to be qualified. Some more questions.
31   How does a team win games?
32 NANCY: A team cops, nips, clobbers, sends reeling to defeat,
33   annexes, licks, repels the highly-touted visitors, romps,
34   shades, ekes out, rides rough-shod over and *(Beats feet*
35   *heavily on floor)* tramples.

1 EDGEWORTH: Fine. What happens when someone hits the
2 ball over the fence?
3 NANCY: When the swatsmith applies the willow to the
4 horsehide and waltzes it out of the ball orchard, he has
5 hit for the circuit, taken the pitcher downtown, blasted
6 a four-master, rapped a round-tripper, hit a four-ply
7 smash or an all-the-way poke.
8 EDGEWORTH: OK. I think you're my new sportswriter.
9 NANCY: *(Closes fist and punches the air, rabid-fan style.)* All
10 *riii*ght!
11 EDGEWORTH: Wait. Couple more things. Baseball has
12 taken some strange twists lately. A few more questions.
13 NANCY: *(Confidently)* Question away.
14 EDGEWORTH: What is collective bargaining?
15 NANCY: *(Puzzled)* What?
16 EDGEWORTH: A contract based on attendance figures?
17 NANCY: Pardon?
18 EDGEWORTH: Wage scale clause?
19 NANCY: Golly . . . I don't know . . .
20 EDGEWORTH: Free agency?
21 NANCY: Don't think I know . . .
22 EDGEWORTH: Federal mediation at the conference table
23 where both sides accuse each other of bargaining in bad
24 faith?
25 NANCY: *(Shaking head)* Have no idea . . .
26 EDGEWORTH: Sorry. The game's changing. It's all dollars
27 and cents and high-powered business agents. We don't
28 like it, but that's the way it is. But here, Miss Andrews,
29 take these tickets to the ball game today. Enjoy yourself.
30 *(She takes tickets and stands up.)*
31 NANCY: Thank you. I'll make the trek up to the House That
32 Ruth Built and watch the Bronx Bombers trounce the
33 hapless Bengals from the Motor City in both ends of a
34 twin bill. Good-by and thanks. *(She starts out, waves to
35 EDGEWORTH and exits. EDGEWORTH rises, nods and sits down.)*

1   **EDGEWORTH:** *(Buzzes intercom on desk.)* **Miss Freebish, I**
2   need a baseball writer to cover the "now" diamond scene.
3   Send in that young lady from the Wall Street Journal.
4   Right . . . yeah, this should do it.

5
6
7
8
9
10
11
12
13
14
15
16
17
18
19
20
21
22
23
24
25
26
27
28
29
30
31
32
33
34
35

#2

Drama Critics' Lingo

CAST: ANNOUNCER, male or female; one MALE; one FEMALE.

SETTING: Simple desk setting. The MALE reads the critics' phrases. The FEMALE will define them for the audience.

ANNOUNCER: The job of drama critics is to inform their reading public and help them decide whether or not to lay down their money to see the show. They must inform, entertain and be completely honest in presenting their opinions. And nearly all do that.

But in every calling, a particular type of vocabulary takes hold. Just as sportscasters, CB radio operators, and politicians, drama critics have their own lexicon.

It takes a lot of reading of reviews and serious thought to find out what the critics really mean.

MALE: *(Firmly, making strong statement)* "This play delves into hitherto unexplored areas."

FEMALE: *(Very understanding, knowledgeable, confident)* This play is dirty.

MALE: "Rarely has this controversial subject been treated with such enlightened maturity."

FEMALE: This play is *very* dirty!

MALE: "The drama is honest and courageous."

FEMALE: It's about a group of thespians and their nocturnal play.

MALE: "It's written with force and insight."

FEMALE: The *author* is a thespian who goes out a lot after dark.

MALE: "Shocking, perhaps, but done with searching candor."

FEMALE: Mass taunting and sexual harassment on the job

1   very sympathetically handled.

2 MALE: "Linda Lovely performs with stark realism."

3 FEMALE: After eating a cabbage, radish and onion sandwich

4   much too quickly, she'll hiccough her way into your heart

5   in the second act.

6 MALE: "A meaningful and earthy slice of life."

7 FEMALE: A rotund supermarket cashier struts across the

8   stage in a shocking pink string bikini.

9 MALE: "Explores the human predicament."

10 FEMALE: Her *uncle* puts on the bikini.

11 MALE: "Linda Lovely and Ronald Drake prove an exceptionally

12   talented terpsichorean couple."

13 FEMALE: They lead a chorus of strolling swineherds in a

14   wild knockdown, drag-out, up-tempo waltz.

15 MALE: "The passionate episodes between Linda and Ronald

16   become tedious and could easily have been cut."

17 FEMALE: The critic has his own bachelor pad and stays

18   home a lot.

19 MALE: "The playwright makes no concessions to the

20   audience."

21 FEMALE: He figures they're all as weird as *he* is.

22 MALE: "The play makes a touching plea for human

23   compassion."

24 FEMALE: *(Compassionately)* The message — be tolerant of

25   lawyers, voyeurs, cruel employers, homicidial maniacs

26   and used car salesmen.

27

28

29

30

31

32

33

34

35

1	**#3**
2	
3	**The Intellectual Ghetto**
4	
5	
6	*CAST:* TV show host CARLTON FLIBNER, smooth, confident,
7	pleasant; ABIGAIL DRINCH, feisty woman of about sixty-five.
8	She is quietly determined to further her cause via TV.
9	
10	*SETTING:* TV show interview set-up consisting of two chairs.
11	
12	**CARLTON:** *(To audience)* **Good morning, everyone. Welcome to**
13	**Sunday Morning Intellectual Ghetto which brings you face**
14	**to face with some of the people who make New York City**
15	**what it is today.** *(He turns to face the guest.)*
16	**With us today is Miss Abigail Drinch, head of the**
17	**Society to Preserve Little Old New York. Miss Drinch, glad**
18	**to have you with us.**
19	**ABIGAIL:** **Thank you.**
20	**CARLTON:** **I understand that your group . . .**
21	**ABIGAIL:** **Glad to be here.**
22	**CARLTON:** *(Take at her two-part response)* **Uh . . . yes . . . that you**
23	**people are engaged in a number of projects to help restore**
24	**the sylvan beauty of the New York of long ago.**
25	**ABIGAIL:** **That's it.**
26	**CARLTON:** **Would you care to tell . . .**
27	**ABIGAIL:** *(Continuing her thought)* **. . . in a nutshell.**
28	**CARLTON:** *(Shakes head.)* **. . . tell us about these projects.**
29	**ABIGAIL:** **My pleasure. You see . . .**
30	**CARLTON:** *(Interrupting)* **Perhaps it might be better to talk**
31	**first about the organization itself.**
32	**ABIGAIL:** **Have it your way.**
33	**CARLTON:** **So . . . tell us about your group.**
34	**ABIGAIL:** *(Smiling amiably)* **It's your show.**
35	**CARLTON:** **It was.**

1	ABIGAIL:	Well, we started in a small place on West Broadway
2		many years ago. That was when West Broadway was
3		considered East Broadway and West 4th Street was
4		considered downtown.
5	CARLTON:	It still *is* downtown.
6	ABIGAIL:	*(Going right on)* Our first headquarters was just a
7		little old tin shack with a broken ceiling and no windows.
8	CARLTON:	A humble beginning. Where is your office now?
9	ABIGAIL:	Same place. But we have a window now. It was
10		donated by one of our past members.
11	CARLTON:	Deceased?
12	ABIGAIL:	No. Franklin.
13	CARLTON:	Go on, Miss Drinch.
14	ABIGAIL:	Well . . . that's about it.
15	CARLTON:	Now tell me, Miss Drinch . . .
16	ABIGAIL:	We try to keep New York old. And we feel that an
17		old New York is a clean New York and a clean New York
18		is an old New York.
19	CARLTON:	Simple but forceful truth. What is your main
20		project now?
21	ABIGAIL:	We want to uncover the Minetta Stream.
22	CARLTON:	Isn't that the underground stream that runs
23		under lower Manhattan and empties into the Hudson
24		River?
25	ABIGAIL:	Bosh and double bosh. You listen to some people
26		and you'd think everything empties into the Hudson.
27	CARLTON:	You unearth the Minetta Stream and then what?
28	ABIGAIL:	And then what? Haven't you been listening?
29	CARLTON:	*(Confused)* Miss Drinch, are we missing something
30		here? *(ABIGAIL pats her body, looks down.)*
31	ABIGAIL:	No, I've got everything. How about yourself?
32	CARLTON:	*(A little rattled)* No, I'm fine. Proceed.
33	ABIGAIL:	The Minetta Stream, as we see it, runs a crazy-
34		quilt pattern, starting from Houston Street, up to West
35		23rd Street, over to Fifth Avenue, past the reviewing stand,

1   up to Times Square where it forms a huge lake which
2   encompasses the new Coliseum.
3 CARLTON: And you want to unearth that entire stream?
4 ABIGAIL: That's our hope.
5 CARLTON: A noble undertaking, but wouldn't that . . .
6 ABIGAIL: New York would be much prettier.
7 CARLTON: Uh . . . yes, but wouldn't that require a lot of
8   razing of buildings and tearing up of streets?
9 ABIGAIL: We think we have the solution to that.
10 CARLTON: And what is that solution?
11 ABIGAIL: We'd raze all the buildings and tear up the streets.
12   It's the only way. *(Firmly, striking table or chair arm)* **The**
13   **only way!**
14 CARLTON: *(Dubious about the whole interview)* I must ask you
15   this question, Miss Drinch. Hope you don't mind. How
16   old are you?
17 ABIGAIL: How old am I? *(She does mind.)* What difference
18   does that make?
19 CARLTON: No offense. I just wanted to inject a comment
20   here that I think you're a very sprightly woman for your
21   age.
22 ABIGAIL: If you don't know how old I am, how do you know
23   how sprightly I'm supposed to be?
24 CARLTON: *(Beleaguered)* I mean that you're sprightly for any
25   age. Let me put it that way.
26 ABIGAIL: *(Irritated)* You can put it any way you want to, pal.
27   For my dough you can put it in your hat and drop it out
28   the window.
29 CARLTON: No offense.
30 ABIGAIL: I've been called sprightly by bigger people than
31   you.
32 CARLTON: I suppose. We still have some time left. Can you
33   tell our listeners how the Minetta Stream got its name?
34 ABIGAIL: I don't know. Is that so all-fired important?
35 CARLTON: Well, I thought . . . uh . . . no, it's not. Well, Miss

1   Drinch, thanks for coming here today and I'll be following
2   your fight to get the Minetta Stream uncovered with great
3   interest.
4   ABIGAIL: Do you think you can give us some financial support?
5   CARLTON: We can't. It's not the station's policy.
6   ABIGAIL: Well, how about broadcasting a barrage of
7   scathing attacks on the city officials for being
8   dunderheads.
9   CARLTON: Can't use that word on the air. We'd like to help,
10   but we can't. But we do wish you luck . . .
11 ABIGAIL: *(Standing up)* Luck don't feed the bulldog, pal.
12 CARLTON: But, Miss Drinch . . .
1   ABIGAIL: I'm splitting, pal. I'll hit the Donahue *(Oprah,*
14   *Geraldo — make your choice)* show and pick up some big
15   bucks.
16 CARLTON: *(Standing up as she exits)* Miss Drinch . . .
17 ABIGAIL: *(Firmly)* So long, pal. And thanks for nothing. *(She*
18   *heads out. As she does so, she gives a quick little skip and an*
19   *energetic jump, belying her years.)* Sprightly indeed. *(Turns)*
20   Cheapskate! *(She leaves as CARLTON, hand to forehead, sinks*
21   *sadly into his seat at blackout.)*
22
23
24
25
26
27
28
29
30
31
32
33
34
35

Broadway Spring Camps

CAST: ANNOUNCER, male or female, On-Stage or Off. Female, SALLY — is young, amiable, efficient in her job as reporter of the Broadway spring training scene. Male, plays *four* roles, changing his character and outfit via quick-change. Roles are: CARL Kitchen — Pinteresque type of closed-mouthed character, representative of that playwright's drama. IGGY Hirsute — a cocky, noisy, confident type of rock musical producer who knows it all. Jim WARDEN — quiet, thoughtful producer of prison shows. ANGUS Jeremiad — sad, teary, lugubrious producer of dreary dramas.

SETTING: Customary chair and desk with whatever props the director feels are necessary — hand mike, paper, pens, etc.

ANNOUNCER: **Broadway is the big league of legitimate theater. Seldom does any play make the jump right to the big time. Usually there is a long, arduous training period, long hours of rehearsal, severe editing and much rewriting if a play is to get ready for the Broadway stage. Those are the reasons for Broadway spring training camps.**

Here are reports from the various camps by our critic Sally Swift with her interviews and outlooks for the numerous plays preparing for Broadway.

(OPENING: SALLY is at desk with guest, CARL Kitchen.)

SALLY: **Our first report is from Pinter City, Florida, and we will talk to the leader of the camp, Coach Carl Kitchen. According to reports, Coach Kitchen hopes to hit three or four of the eight plays on his roster. Some of the titles are "Some Old Times," "Very Good Times," "Good Times**

1   Sometimes," "Times Ain't Too Bad," "New Times Is Awful
2   Times" and "How's Your Uncle's Birthmark?" Is that
3   about it, Carl? *(Hesitates thoughtfully.)*
4 CARL: Mmmm...
5 SALLY: I know you don't recognize me. I'm Sally Swift from
6   the press.
7 CARL: Mmmm?
8 SALLY: The press.
9 CARL: Yes... the press.
10 SALLY: I'm here to...
11 CARL: Not here last year?
12 SALLY: No. I...
13 CARL: What happened to the other...?
14 SALLY: Married.
15 CARL: Love?
16 SALLY: Some.
17 CARL: Dreary.
18 SALLY: Somewhat.
19 CARL: Mmmm...
20 SALLY: Season look good?
21 CARL: Mayhaps.
22 SALLY: Dramas?
23 CARL: Stark.
24 SALLY: Successful?
25 CARL: Quite.
26 SALLY: Mmmm... Thank you, Carl Kitchen.
27 CARL: Hmmm... *(He exits, shambling out slowly.)*
28 SALLY: Our outlook — if prolix playwrights can truncate
29   verbosity, group could accumulate all the marbles and
30   wave the gonfalon proudly.
31   *(Stage can go dark momentarily giving male performer time to*
32   *change quickly into next character. SALLY is seated at desk, on*
33   *stage alone.)*
34 SALLY: *(Continued)* Here in Little Musical Rock, Arkansas,
35   nudity and profanity ride rampant as gawky youngsters

1   **go through their paces in putting together one-word hits.**
2   **We're going to be talking to company manager Iggy "Hot**
3   **Rock" Hirsute.** *(IGGY comes in garishly dressed, with long*
4   *beard and possibly wearing horn-rimmed glasses. He is sure of*
5   *himself, a know-it-all — sleazy and slimy are what he is. He*
6   *plops down on a chair.)* **You've had three hits, Iggy — Grip,**
7   **Fig and Stump — all running at an Off-off-off-off Broadway**
8   **cabin. Fargo, North Dakota, to be precise.**
9   **IGGY:**   **That's the place you start 'em.**
10 **SALLY:**   **What is the secret of your success?**
11 **IGGY:**   **We strip away the hypocrisy that binds the archaic**
12   **American morality without desecrating a human's**
13   **impulse, using only fundamentally base elements.**
14 **SALLY:**   **What are these elements?**
15 **IGGY:**   **No plot. No clothes. Loud music. We slap the**
16   **establishment, hit organized religion and degrade**
17   **romance in a healthy, open manner. We get the audience**
18   **involved by tickling their risibilities, rubbing their necks**
19   **and mentally disrobing them in a meaningful way.**
20 **SALLY:**   **Some say the public is getting tired of this.**
21 **IGGY:**   **Our audiences never tire of vulgarity. We use six-**
22   **letter curse words and this year we're introducing a**
23   **twenty-one-letter, multisyllable obscenity that will**
24   **shatter your self-respect.**
25 **SALLY:**   **May I hear it?**
26 **IGGY:**   **No out-of-town previews.**
27 **SALLY:**   *(Trying to provoke him)* **Why you dirty, rotten little . . .**
28   *(IGGY eyes her, turns and leaves quickly as stage goes dark.)*
29   *(Lights come up and SALLY is seated alone at desk.)*
30 **SALLY:**   *(Continued)* **Here in the state penitentiary at**
31   **Recidivist, Kansas, under the watchful eyes of gun-**
32   **bearing guards atop a watchtower, lifers, drifters,**
33   **gunmen, bank robbers and assorted killers are tapping**
34   **out plays of prison life, hoping to break out to financial**
35   **freedom.**

1   **Famous hoods such as Heat-Head Harold, who killed**
2   **eight plumbers with three probables; Lenny Loosener,**
3   **who led the mid-West circuit in stolen vases, and**
4   **Rollicking Rolly Nerfin, famed playboy who was arrested**
5   **three times for kissing with intent to harm, are busy**
6   **working on plays about crime, prison life and being**
7   **behind bars.** *(Coach Jim WARDEN comes in and sits down.*
8   *He is calm, dressed in a conservative outfit.)* **What's the**
9   **outlook, Coach Warden?**
10 **WARDEN:**   Well, Sally, it looks like it's going to be even more
11   violent than last year when seventy-eight front row
12   audience members suffered powder burns.
13 **SALLY:**   Any special plays we should keep an eye out for?
14 **WARDEN:**   Well, we're trying to find one just like, "We Miss
15   You on the Outside, Rocky," which ran for eight months
16   — with two weeks off for good behavior.
17 **SALLY:**   Any particular favorites?
18 **WARDEN:**   We're readying "Moll Flanders — Gangster's
19   Girl," "Who Stole My Cookies?" and "They Died Belching,"
20   about a revenge-ridden chef who vents his pique at fellow
21   inmates by putting explosive pellets in their caviar.
22 **SALLY:**   Thank you, Coach Warden. *(He nods and heads off.)*
23   Season outlook — fine year ahead for squad that can
24   deliver great escape entertainment.
25   *(Lights down. When they come up, SALLY is alone at desk.)*
26 **SALLY:**   *(Continued)* **From Beckett's Pass, Arizona — on the**
27   **barren flatlands of this desert town, a half-dozen**
28   **companies are getting prepared for that fall journey to**
29   **the big town's brightest lights. Despondency, gloom and**
30   **unceasing pessimism about the human condition abound**
31   **here, in keeping with the general tone of the plays being**
32   **put together. You see sobbing stage crews setting up pale**
33   **backgrounds and cardboard props to heighten the aura**
34   **of despair. Misery prevails. Sadness runs riot. Performers**
35   **sit in partially filled garbage cans, flipping twist-off tops**

1	from diet soda bottles, bemoaning society's fate. *(ANGUS*
2	*Jeremiad comes in very slowly, he is dabbing his eyes with a*
3	*handkerchief. We may even hear a slight sob or two.)* **This is**
4	**Angus Jeremiad, the man in charge of the proceedings**
5	**out here. What's in store this year, Angus?**
6	ANGUS: *(Sniffing a bit)* **We have a great crop of crybabies this**
7	**year. We got a bonus whimperer from Sweden who can**
8	**take us all the way. I'm talking about a whiner who comes**
9	**through with racking sobs that will shake the balcony.**
10	**Moan? Not since Libby Holman sang the blues.** *(His voice*
11	*gets mournful as he goes on.)* **Lugubrious overtones with**
12	**delicate shadings of moral decay, as always, are our goals.**
13	**Sadness, moroseness, hopelessness reigns. We**
14	**reflect life. Life reflects art. What is art? Gloom with**
15	**production values. After all, whither goest doom?** *(He sobs*
16	*a bit and is silent.)*
17	SALLY: *(Bubbly)* **Outlook — optimistic, great, bubbly, looking**
18	**up. Observers see another happy, fun-filled, profitable,**
19	**big bonanza bucks year.**
20	ANGUS: *(Looking up suddenly)* **You think so? Big bucks?**
21	SALLY **That's the way most folks see it. I'm happy for you.**
22	ANGUS: *(Standing up happily)* **Great. Happiness brings the**
23	**big bucks. I can get that Rolls. Thank you, Sally. You've**
24	**made my day!** *(He does a happy, little-boy skip and exits quickly.*
25	*SALLY smiles happily as the stage goes dark.)*
26	
27	
28	
29	
30	
31	
32	
33	
34	
35	

#5

Classic Movie Clichés —
And What Followed Them

CAST: ANNOUNCER, male or female, On-Stage or Off; one BOY; one GIRL.

ANNOUNCER: Every television late night movie fan knows the time-honored film clichés that have become ingrained in our memories. Classics like *(With excitement)* "Stop the presses! I've got a story that will blow this town wide open!" and *(Pleading)* "Tell me, doctor, will Old Jeb pull through?" will be with us forever.

But who remembers the lines of dialog or the action immediately following these gems?

For all you film trivia buffs, we'd like to present to you just what happened after the all-time favorite movie clichés.

(BOY and GIRL come out. They can be holding scripts and read their lines if desired. They can stand or be seated at a table.)

BOY: Can't you see I'm trying to help you?

GIRL: But I don't *need* the Heimlich Maneuver.

GIRL: But, Lefty, what was I supposed to do? They told me you were dead . . .

BOY: What are you talking about? I was only gone twenty minutes.

GIRL: But why am I telling all this to you . . . a perfect stranger?

BOY: Boy, now you've really flipped it. We've been married twenty-eight years!

1   GIRL: *(Tough voice)* **We have ways of making you talk.**
2   BOY: *(Speech impediment)* **I ... cer ... cert ... cert ... certainly**
3   **ho-ho-hope so.**
4
5   GIRL: **Mr. Drear, I know this has been a terrible ordeal for**
6   **you and how nervous and uptight you must be, but will**
7   **you please tell the jury exactly what happened the night**
8   **of February 17th ... Mr. Drear ... Mr. Drear ...** *(Turning)*
9   **Bailiff, will you please wake up the witness?**
10
11   BOY: **Who are you trying to protect?**
12   GIRL: **It's not who, stupid! It's whom! Gee, don't they teach**
13   **these kids anything these days?**
14
15   BOY: **No one has even broken out of this place.**
16   GIRL: **I know. I heard the principal** *(Dean)* **is a light sleeper.**
17
18
19   GIRL: **Well, it's out of our hands now.**
20   BOY: **Yeah, and all over my vest.** *(Calling)* **Waiter, get me a**
21   **towel.**
22
23   GIRL: *(Seriously)* **If we could just try it out on a human being.**
24   BOY: *(Moronic)* **Dah ... well ... dat lets me out.**
25
26   BOY: **Boy, you explorers are something. Ma'am, you've been**
27   **out on this desert for three days. Here, drink this water.**
28   GIRL: **Did you let it run?**
29
30   BOY: **We have a part for you in a big Broadway musical, but**
31   **we can't use your partner.**
32   GIRL: **But we're Siamese twins.**
33
34   BOY: **Of course you're scared. We're** *all* **scared, kid.**
35   GIRL: **This your first visit to New York, too?**

1   **BOY:**   **Why, Miss Jones, I've never seen you without your**

2   **glasses . . . or your hat . . . or overcoat . . . or galoshes . . .**

3   **or hearing aid . . . or electric cummerbund.**

4

5   **GIRL:**   *(Cooly)* **Don't turn around. Don't look back. I want to**

6   **remember you just the way you are.** *(BOY turns his face or*

7   *walks away from her. She uses her fingers as a gun and fires,*

8   *making appropriate sound. BOY turns back or walks back to*

9   *her, dying.)*

10   **BOY:**   *(Puzzled, pleading)* **Why . . . why did you do it?**

11   **GIRL:**   *(With great fervor)* **Oh, John. Can't you see I'm trying to**

12   **tell you that I love you?** *(BOY and GIRL sit together and face*

13   *audience.)*

14   **BOY and GIRL:**   *(Unison)* **D-d-d-d-dat's all, folks.**

15

16

17

18

19

20

21

22

23

24

25

26

27

28

29

30

31

32

33

34

35

6

Want to Be a Writer? — Do the Write Thing

CAST: ANNOUNCER, male or female, On-Stage or Off. BEN, polite, bookish; AMY, fits just about the same description. They should be dressed conservatively, possibly each wearing horn-rimmed glasses.

SETTING: Desk or table with two chairs. Desk might contain several magazines which can be referred to by the performers. They also can have their scripts inside the magazine for easy reference or reading.

ANNOUNCER: **There are many people out there who want to write. Everyone feels he or she has a story deep inside just waiting to burst out. Well, don't be timid. Sit down and write! Now, you can't expect to start at the top, but there are plenty of magazines eager to read, print and pay for your manuscripts. There are several publications willing to buy from beginners. So get busy and write! Amy? Ben? Will you tip us off about where the action is for young writers?**

AMY: **We certainly will.**

BEN: **Here's a note from Stanley Sagebrush, editor of Wildcat Westerns.** *(Reads)* **"We want horse stories and we want them horsey. No sidesaddle stuff for us."**

AMY: **Payment is a flat twenty-five dollars per tale.**

BEN: **Or, in this case, per tail. As in horse's.**

AMY: **Very good, Ben.**

BEN: **We want no trite plots such as the rancher's illiterate daughter rescuing her fiancé's pet cobra from the village slaughterhouse.**

AMY: **Been done to death.**

1	BEN:	Love should be kept to a minimum.
2	AMY:	*(Winning smile)* You know that as well as we do.
3	BEN:	Send stories to Box 15, Saddlesore, Texas.
4	AMY:	Geologist's Weekly — Fred Cro-Magnon, editor.
5	BEN:	"We want funny essays concerning life in the Dark
6		Ages ...
7	AMY:	Also known as the "Roaring Twenties."
8	BEN:	We will pay three cents a chuckle.
9	AMY:	Chuckle sampler sent on request.
10	BEN:	Send your yocks and boffs to us at 222 Diversey Street,
11		Deepdown, Oklahoma.
12	AMY:	*(Strong voice)* Fierce Detective!
13	BEN:	Minnie Mayhem, editor.
14	AMY:	And what is Minnie looking for, Ben?
15	BEN:	"We are a big market for stories of murder, stranglings
16		of a tasteful nature, and assorted crimes committed by
17		shorter-than-average bad people. We also like high-type
18		misdemeanors, the kind the family can read together."
19	AMY:	Example of what we like — "The Sweetest Gory Ever
20		Told" — in our June issue.
21	BEN:	No multiple fracture stories.
22	AMY:	Just good, solid down-to-earth crime — with a twist.
23	BEN:	We pay two cents a word — at gunpoint.
24	AMY:	Mail scripts to Binger Street, Bangor, Maine.
25	BEN:	The Working Plumber.
26	AMY:	Edmund Plunger, editor.
27	BEN:	"Any article presenting problems encountered by the
28		everyday plumber is welcomed."
29	AMY:	Stories of bent pipes, rusty sidings, weather-beaten
30		wrenches and ugly pets who nip when plumbers are bent
31		in unusual positions.
32	BEN:	That's what we're looking for.
33	AMY:	We do not pay, but hope someday to thank you
34		personally.
35	BEN:	And maybe send a box of chocolate nougats around the

1   holidays.
2   AMY: No offbeat stuff for Working Plumber. We're strictly
3   mainstream.
4   BEN: Address manuscripts to Subterranean City, Swamp
5   County, Florida.
6   AMY: Crossword Puzzles Monthly.
7   BEN: Black and White, editors.
8   AMY: We love puzzles that keep people going around in
9   squares.
10 BEN: Be careful of the type of words you use as we are a
11   family publication.
12 AMY: Taboo — three-syllable synonyms for bad things in
13   general.
14 BEN: We are currently putting together our largest issue, an
15   anniversary special commemorating our late editor,
16   Harold Syntax, who died last week.
17 AMY: He was buried six down and three across.
18 BEN: Send puzzles to Box 1, Anagram, Ohio.
19 AMY: Sordid Confessions.
20 BEN: Harry Libertine, editor.
21 AMY: Send us your own personal experiences and we may
22   buy them at three cents a gasp.
23 BEN: Anything cheap, trashy, nasty or just plain rotten is
24   right up our alley.
25 AMY: Use real names as it will create greater interest in your
26   hometown.
27 BEN: If stories are off-color we will pay four cents a word.
28 AMY: If very sordid, we go up to five cents a word.
29 BEN: If they are unbelievably off-color, our editor Harry
30   Libertine will pay ten cents a word and move in with you.
31 AMY: Send scripts to Tell It Like It Is, Squealer, Kansas.
32 BEN: When it comes to sordid and gamey —
33 **AMY and BEN:**   *(Unison, putting their hands behind ears and*
34   *pushing forward)* **We're all ears!**
35

#7

The Big Boomer in Today's Literature —
The Romance Novel

CAST: ANNOUNCER, male or female; Novelist, ZACK Whistler; Editor, GWEN Farrady. Both are in their thirties or forties; both are attractive people.

SETTING: Desk, chair in which GWEN Farrady is seated.

ANNOUNCER: Without a doubt, the biggest rage in publishing today is the romance novel.

> **These tomes are presided over chiefly by astute lady editors and are churned out regularly by female writers — for the most part.**

> **We now know that some men write romance novels under a woman's pseudonym.**

> **Let's look in now as a male writer tries his hand at cracking this lush market. His job? To read the opening of his novel to a knowing, experienced editor in the romance field. He hopes to impress her enough to be offered a contract for the book.**

(ZACK paces the floor nervously, glancing and mouthing some of his words, as he prepares to read for the editor.)

GWEN: Anytime you're ready, Mr. Whistler.

ZACK: Right. *(Clears his throat for quite a long while, trying to rev up his nerve to read aloud.)*

GWEN: Would you like to gargle?

ZACK: No. I'm fine.

GWEN: This your first time?

ZACK: Yes ... this is my first time. First time.

GWEN: *(Pleasantly)* **Relax. I'll be gentle.**

ZACK: Thank you. *(Begins reading.)* **"Kisses in the Gloaming ..."**

1   GWEN: *(Repeating questioningly)* **"Kisses in the Gloaming?"**

2   **Well . . . we'll work on it.** *(ZACK paces nervously as he reads.)*

3   ZACK: **"Kisses in the Gloaming" by Esmeralda Graybeard.**

4   GWEN: *(Coming alive)* **Esmeralda Graybeard?! Sounds too**

5   **old. We try to keep things youthful. Make it Lolita Nubile.**

6   ZACK: *(Repeating)* **Lolita Nubile. Right.** *(Reads)* **As the rising**

7   **sun poked its inquisitive head into the north window of**

8   **the old Grippaloo mansion, a graceful alabaster arm**

9   **reached out of the perfumed, silken bedcovers and**

10   **lingeringly caressed the fleshy, curving skin of Angela**

11   **Lowdown's left ankle.** *(Upstage, GWEN, unseen by ZACK,*

12   *sets action to his words, caressing her left ankle. GWEN can*

13   *really ham up all her actions.)* **Out of her carefully molded**

14   **mouth came a melodious yawn.** *(GWEN begins a yawn and*

15   *stifles it with a hurried move of her hand.)* **She ran fingers**

16   **through her glowing tresses and slithered neatly into an**

17   **upright position.** *(GWEN does so, sitting suddenly as ZACK*

18   *turns.)* **Her one hundred twenty-five pounds of tortuous**

19   **beauty were only a whisper upon her gently curving**

20   **heels. Slowly, almost sensuously, she reaches down to**

21   **touch her gently curving toes, a morning ritual to help**

22   **keep her luscious frame lean and lissome.** *(GWEN stands,*

23   *does so, stopping quickly and sitting again as ZACK looks toward*

24   *her.)* **True to her sex, Angela gazed at her loveliness in**

25   **the mirror,** *(GWEN stares at herself in her compact mirror)*

26   **inspecting every pore of her gently curving cheekbones.**

27   *(GWEN touches her cheekbones.)* **Though she had slept only**

28   **four hours, her eyes were eager and alert** *(GWEN widens*

29   *her eyes)* **and ready for another tussle on the battlefield**

30   **of love.** *(ZACK looks at her.)*

31   GWEN: *(Nodding approvingly)* **You're on a roll, keep it moving.**

32   ZACK: **On her forehead was a small smear, a momento of a**

33   **hectic evening at the archduke's ball. It was an**

34   **unavoidable accident, thought Angela, as she recalled**

35   **how the duke had singed her with his cigar when he put**

1   **his hand across her gently curving face to crush his lips**
2   **upon hers.** *(GWEN, eyes open wide, rubs her fingers on her*
3   *lips.)* **But the duke missed and he fell off the chair.** *(GWEN*
4   *snaps her fingers in disappointment. ZACK goes on with the*
5   *story.)* **But what's a cigar burn when your heart is**
6   **exploding in flames?** *(GWEN shrugs "it's nothing.")* **"Oh,**
7   **what an evening,"** Angela sighed. *(GWEN does so.)* **Soft**
8   **music, romantic surroundings, artichoke hearts and the**
9   **duke. Gently curving duke.** *(GWEN, puzzled at this, mouths*
10   *"gentle curving duke?")* **Angela looked into the mirror**
11   *(GWEN does so)* **and gazed at her miraculously even teeth**
12   **which stood like rigid ballerinas on a sturdy plateau.**
13   *(GWEN does so, examining her teeth. ZACK turns to her.)* **Is**
14   **that real? The teeth bit?**
15 GWEN: Oh, sure. We chicks like to check our chops.
16 ZACK: *(Going on)* **Then, returning to the world of reality, she**
17   **straightened suddenly and tore the diaphanous gown**
18   **from her gently curving body.** *(GWEN stands up suddenly,*
19   *grasps the top of her blouse and makes motion to rip it off. She*
20   *catches herself, shakes her head in dismay.)* **There she stood,**
21   **naked to the world.** *(GWEN, caught up, goes into a blushing,*
22   *shy caricature of September Morn.)* **She stayed this way three**
23   **hours.**
24 GWEN: Three hours?! Standing like this . . . like this . . . like
25   that? No way! Unreal. An hour-and-a-quarter maybe. Not
26   three hours. Go on.
27 ZACK: **Suddenly she raised her arms above her, twirled**
28   **slowly curving arms in a circle,** *(GWEN, unseen by ZACK,*
29   *does so)* **and folded her gently curving arms in front of**
30   **her to caress each shoulder.** *(GWEN does so, mugging more*
31   *than a little.)* **There was a call. On the balcony across the**
32   **courtyard was the duke, who was so entranced by the**
33   **lovely vision of the gently curving Angela, he dropped**
34   **his binoculars. He called in that familiar mellifluous**
35   **voice, "Hey, Angela, want to go to the turtle races today?"**

1	**"Yes, yes,"Angela replied. "Dad said I could use the horse.**
2	**Pick you up at three."** *(GWEN gives the OK sign with circled*
3	*index finger and thumb.)* **Then the duke was gone. A look**
4	**of dreaminess overtook Angela. She closed her gently**
5	**curving eyes and then opened them** *(GWEN does so)* **as**
6	**she gazed up at the alabaster ceiling.** *(GWEN leans back*
7	*in chair and does so.)* **But why live in the past? Tonight was**
8	**ahead.** *(GWEN brightens up, smiling with anticipation.)*
9	**Tonight would be an even greater, more fulfilling**
10	**excursion into the delights of rapturous ecstasy. Angela**
11	**leaped up** *(GWEN does so, clicking her heels joyously)* **and**
12	**bounded out of the gently curving bedroom to prepare**
13	**for another night of enchantment, love, excitement,**
14	**love** . . . *(ZACK paces as he continues, not seeing GWEN behind*
15	*him, who does the cheerleader's clenched fist jab of approval with*
16	*each word from ZACK)* . . . **romance, love,** *(ZACK's voice gets*
17	*louder)* **tenderness . . . passion . . .** *love! (Exhausted, GWEN*
18	*sinks back into her chair. Then she straightens up, business-like,*
19	*completely the professional editor as ZACK approaches.)* **Well?**
20	GWEN: *(Firmly)* **Sorry. Won't go. No reader identification.**
21	*(ZACK registers disappointment, then, shoulders drooping,*
22	*trudges off slowly as GWEN busies herself with some papers.*
23	*She looks at the departing ZACK, smiles a look of "well,*
24	*maybe . . ." then shakes her head "no" and goes back to work.*
25	*Curtain or blackout.)*
26	
27	
28	
29	
30	
31	
32	
33	
34	
35	

Bonnie and Clyde Agency for the Unemployed Underworld

CAST: ANNOUNCER, male or female, On-Stage or Off. BONNIE, attractive, gun-moll type; CLYDE, her partner who looks as if he knows his way around crime circles . . . and he does.

SETTING: Desk or table with two chairs in a TV studio. Papers or pads which performers can read script from or refer to from time to time.

ANNOUNCER: We all know there are specialized employment agencies for various fields. You see the ads for waitresses, bookkeepers, editors, architects, typists, etcetera. But to the best of our knowledge there is only one agency specializing in getting work for members of the underworld — the Bonnie and Clyde Agency for the Unemployed Underworld.
(OPENING: BONNIE and CLYDE are seated across from each other or side by side at the table or desk. They have their notes on pads in front of them.

BONNIE: Attention, crooks, stick-up artists, pickpockets and strong-armed men. Reached a dead end? At the stage where you don't know where your next meal ticket is coming from?

CLYDE: Then this announcement is for you.

BONNIE: We may have a position available that could be right down your dark alley.

CLYDE: The Bonnie and Clyde Agency has in its files administrative positions for experienced planners of bank heists.

BONNIE: Two of our people are winners of the Heistman's

1   Trophy.
2   CLYDE: We can find openings for you beginning house-
3   breakers at the entry level.
4   BONNIE: Some of the people we have helped include Dipper
5   Marigold, ex-rubber hose man for a timid police sergeant.
6   CLYDE: Ripper Donleavy, famed extortionist, who is now
7   operating a successful bullet farm in upstate New York.
8   BONNIE: Moll Flanders, lookout, gun bearer and downright
9   flirt, who provided diversionary tactics during a whole
10   string of successful wishing well robberies.
11 CLYDE: We can get work for you. This is how we operate.
12 BONNIE: Attention all you syndicate chiefs, gang lords,
13   would-be crime executives and just plain citizens, listen
14   as we tell you of our clients seeking new employment
15   opportunities.
16 CLYDE: Bonnie and Clyde can help with your personnel
17   difficulties.
18 BONNIE: To the regional syndicate boss:
19 CLYDE: Looking for a good number two man in your
20   operation? "Bugs" Whitlaw is just that man.
21 BONNIE: A veteran of four running gun battles with Chicago
22   police, Bugs has, at this very moment, two police chiefs
23   and one state legislator under his thumb.
24 CLYDE: Bugs masterminded the famous Skokie, Illinois,
25   bank job netting $2,034,253 after taxes, a record for the
26   midwest region that still stands.
27 BONNIE: A positive magician at employee relations, no one
28   ever quit a job on Bugs. Several have disappeared under
29   mysterious circumstances, but none has ever quit.
30 CLYDE: A native of Hammond, Indiana, Bugs is a graduate
31   of Larry Fagan's Larceny Institute. He is a nonsmoker,
32   likes tall women and shoots in the low forties.
33 BONNIE: However, he is willing to shoot anyone if the price
34   is right.
35 CLYDE: Client number two.

1   BONNIE: Just a brief note here to introduce Piggy Stiles, a
2   raffish young man with an ingratiating sense of humor,
3   who is rapidly building up a fine local reputation as a
4   pickpocket-about-town.
5   CLYDE: Despite his tender years, Piggy can turn an afternoon
6   at a Turkish bath, carnival, tennis game or tea room, into
7   a profitable venture.
8   BONNIE: He's going places, this lad, and I, for one, have
9   placed a "can't miss" label on him.
10   CLYDE: Act now — let *his* fingers do the walking for your mob.
11   BONNIE: And now, client number three.
12   CLYDE: To those of you out there, bad people and upstanding
13   citizens alike, who are vindictive and revenge-ridden,
14   but without means or strength to retaliate against a real
15   or fancied humiliation — this may be for you.
16   BONNIE: Ever thought of adopting a mad killer?
17   CLYDE: If not, listen. This may change your mind.
18   BONNIE: Think of it. There's someone you dislike. You are
19   powerless to get even. Not a pleasant scenario, is it?
20   CLYDE: Of course it isn't. But there is a solution.
21   BONNIE: Simply antagonize this mad killer and sic him
22   onto the troublemaker who's been ruining your life. Yes,
23   relief is just a moment away.
24   CLYDE: This mad killer, of course, will eventually be
25   apprehended, committed, incarcerated or annihilated as
26   the case may be, but your hands are clean.
27   BONNIE: You can walk proud and tall in the sun once more.
28   CLYDE: We have just such a mad killer registered with us.
29   BONNIE: Name sent on request.
30   CLYDE: He's a hypersensitive young man with powerful
31   forearms who grits his teeth something awful when
32   irritated.
33   BONNIE: He is woefully disturbed and terribly anxiety-ridden.
34   CLYDE: It shouldn't take too much to set him off the deep
35   end and get to work for you. He has a fine track record.

1   BONNIE: Names of previous victims sent on request.

2   CLYDE: Won't you do yourself and a misguided maniac a favor

3   by taking him under your wing until the time is ripe?

4   BONNIE: Why not open up your heart and let this mad killer

5   in?

6   CLYDE: Before we sign off, we'd like to remind all our

7   viewers out there to be good to your employees in the

8   underworld.

9   BONNIE: Remember our motto — Crime doesn't pay…

10   enough.

11

12

13

14

15

16

17

18

19

20

21

22

23

24

25

26

27

28

29

30

31

32

33

34

35

#9

Pickup in the Park

CAST: DON, CAROL — both are young, from late teens to midtwenties. They are dressed in average contemporary street clothes.

SETTING: Park bench at midday. CAROL is seated on the bench reading a newspaper. DON comes along, starts to pass, then catches a glimpse of her and stops, hesitates, then approaches.

DON: *(Politely)* **May I sit here with you?** *(CAROL looks him over for a few seconds, then gives a slow, twirling motion with her right hand, arm extended. DON is puzzled. He repeats her motion. She nods. He points to himself.)* **Me?** *(Twirls hand as she has done. She nods. He shrugs, steps back and twirls in a circle slowly. He then approaches bench.)* **Well?** *(She shakes her head "no" and goes back to her paper. Stunned, DON rushes to the bench and sits down. She hastily bounces away toward the end of the bench.)* **Now that wasn't fair. Making me do that. What am I, on inspection?**

CAROL: **I'm a comparison shopper.**

DON: **You're not buying me . . . nobody *buys* me. You had me spinning around out there like a fool. I felt like a piece of meat on a rack . . . a spinning rack . . . out there for you to judge.**

CAROL: **If I were indeed judging, you wouldn't be rated prime cut.**

DON: **Is that so?**

CAROL: **Not the way you've been needling me.**

DON: **Needling you? Look, you gave me a suggestion to do something and I did it.**

CAROL: **Not a suggestion . . . an order.**

1   DON: You admit it! Just because I'm a male you took
2   advantage and ordered me to do something.
3   CAROL: And you did it.
4   DON: That's sexual harassment.
5   CAROL: That only happens on the job. And you're not
6   working. Probably don't even have a job.
7   DON: I've got a job. A good job. Steady job. Good future.
8   CAROL: Is this a paid commercial announcement?
9   DON: All I'm saying is that I'm working. This is my lunch
10   break.
11   CAROL: Do you spend all your lunch hours stalking the
12   grounds, looking for innocent victims?
13   DON: Hey, a guy's gotta do what a guy's gotta do. Of course I
14   don't stalk.
15   CAROL: *(Tough girl talk)* **So, you won't stalk, eh?** *(Giggles)*
16   DON: That's funny. Get a job as a clown somewhere . . .
17   instead of sitting around alone on a park bench waiting
18   to pick up who knows what.
19   CAROL: *(Rising to this)* **Pick up? Me? Pick up?**
20   DON: *(Grunting, ape-man style)* **Me, Tarzan** . . . *(Pointing to her)*
21   **You pickup.** *(They pause for a second, look at each other and*
22   *both laugh. They're both more comfortable now.)*
23   CAROL: Well, maybe you're not half bad after all. You *could*
24   put on a little weight.
25   DON: I'm just right for my height. But you look like you
26   could . . .
27   CAROL: What? Could what?
28   DON: Nothing . . . don't change a thing. Don't lose a . . . it's
29   nice . . . it's all right. Everything. The way you smile, your
30   hair, the way you walk and talk . . .
31   CAROL: You've never seen me walk.
32   DON: I can dream can't I? Even park stalkers have dreams.
33   CAROL: *(Smiles)* **Well** . . . yes . . . maybe I could shift a few
34   pounds around.
35   DON: That's entirely up to you. I see no need for any pound

1 shifting.

2 CAROL: If you say so, then I'll stay put. Say, you're not such
3 a bad guy, really. Let's have another look.

4 DON: What kind of look? *(She twirls her hand around as she did*
5 *before. He repeats movement, dumbfounded.)* No, no. Not again.
6 Not me.

7 CAROL: One more time. You could make a few brownie
8 points with me.

9 DON: Never. *(She shrugs and goes back to reading her newspaper.)*
10 OK . . . just once. *(He reluctantly stands up and slowly moves*
11 *away. Even more slowly he starts to twirl.)*

12 CAROL: *(Looking off and calling out)* It's all right, folks. He's
13 with me.

14 DON: *(Through clenched teeth)* I'm beginning to feel a little silly.

15 CAROL: You're beginning to look *very* silly. I'm going to
16 pretend I don't even know you. *(DON rushes back and sits*
17 *down next to her.)*

18 DON: But you *don't* know me.

19 CAROL: More's the shame of it.

20 DON: That's right. And I don't know you. *(Looks at watch.)* And
21 I only have twenty minutes left to stalk. Hey, I'm OK. Get
22 to know me. Try me, you'll like me.

23 CAROL: Twenty minutes, eh? OK, what's your name?

24 DON: Don. And yours?

25 CAROL: Don Andyours? Is that French-Canadian?

26 DON: Don. Call me Don. That's my first name. What is your
27 name?

28 CAROL: Carol.

29 DON: Ah, now we're getting somewhere.

30 CAROL: Just where are we getting?

31 DON: I don't know . . . I get the feeling I'm just spinning my
32 wheels.

33 CAROL: I would say so.

34 DON: I mean I came over here with all good intentions, trying
35 to charm you . . .

1   CAROL: Charm? Seduce is the word.

2   DON: I like charm.

3   CAROL: I like ... no ... forget that ... what do you do at
4   work?

5   DON: *(Relaxing now)* Bank. Junior officer. When girls hear I
6   work in a bank, they begin to show interest in me.

7   CAROL: How about that, folks? A joking banker.

8   DON: Not really a banker, just a junior officer.

9   CAROL: A joking junior officer banker.

10   DON: Now you've got it. What do you do?

11   CAROL: Librarian.

12   DON: I should have known. Your smile speaks volumes.

13   CAROL: And still they come. I like a witty man. Do you know
14   where I could find one?

15   DON: It's just that pretty women inspire me to humorous
16   heights.

17   CAROL: Is that here in town?

18   DON: Aha! Now you're doing it. I think we'd hit it off quite
19   well.

20   CAROL: *(Shrugs, looking at him)* Well ...

21   DON: But then ... I'm an old-fashioned guy. And you're
22   packed away with all those books about every subject in
23   the entire world. You're probably way ahead of me, living
24   a wilder, more knowledgeable, more memorable type of
25   life.

26   CAROL: *(Looks again.)* It's possible.

27   DON: I'm just a simple guy. Straight arrow. Upright. Decent.
28   No wild man me. I believe in marriage. Do you?

29   CAROL: Do I what?

30   DON: Go waterskiing at midnight? Do you believe in
31   marriage is what I want to know.

32   CAROL: Yes ... if it's a lasting one.

33   DON: There you go. We *do* have something in common.

34   CAROL: None of this three and four marches down the aisle
35   stuff.

1 DON: One trip only. Two by two.

2 CAROL: Side by side.

3 DON: You for me.

4 CAROL: Man and wife.

5 DON: Forever.

6 CAROL: Through thick and thin.

7 DON: Through storm and strife.

8 CAROL: Man is the husband.

9 DON: Woman the wife. *(They pause and look at each other fondly.)*

10 CAROL: And we'd never see anyone else.

11 DON: Won't see anybody else ever. *(They pause and look at each*

12 *other, then CAROL turns away, smiles happily and waves. DON*

13 *does the same.)*

14 CAROL: *(Calling)* **Jim!** *(She gets up and exits.)*

15 DON: *(Calling)* **Shirley!** *(He gets up and leaves. Curtain.)*

16

17

18

19

20

21

22

23

24

25

26

27

28

29

30

31

32

33

34

35

#10

Did She or Didn't She?

6 *CAST:* ANNOUNCER, male or female, On-Stage or Off. Young
7   MAN, young LADY.

8
9 *SETTING:* An electric chair with a switch, either attached or nearby.
10 *PROPS:* The switch and some straps and a headpiece for the MAN
11   in the chair.

12
13 ANNOUNCER: **Many of you will remember the classic short**
14   **story by Frank Stockton called "The Lady or the Tiger?"**
15   **You remember, the handsome young courtier was placed**
16   **in the center of a crowded arena because he had**
17   **attempted a romance with the king's daughter. He faced**
18   **two closed doors. His job — to select one of the two doors.**
19   **Behind one, nothing — it meant his freedom. Behind the**
20   **other — a man-eating tiger. As he stood before the doors**
21   **trying to make his choice before a roaring crowd at jam-**
22   **packed Tiger Stadium, the beautiful princess gave him**
23   **a signal with the wave of her fan. The question — did she**
24   **signal for him to go free and find someone else to love,**
25   **or signal the tiger, for him to be the main course on the**
26   **tiger's menu? Never been decided.**
27   **Choices oftentimes determine the outcome of a**
28   **pivotal situation and decide the future of an individual.**
29   **We want you to judge this same situation. Watch this**
30   **drama/fantasy and decide for yourselves — did she or**
31   **didn't she?**
32   *(OPENING: MAN is sitting in the electric chair. LADY is at the*
33   *switch. She is dawdling, being quite nervous. This is her first*
34   *time at the switch.)*
35 **MAN:** *(Impatiently)* **Let's get on with it, shall we?**

1   LADY: OK, OK, you're not going anywhere.
2   MAN: Yeah, but the suspense is killing me.
3   LADY: Suspense and ten thousand volts ... if I ever get this
4   damn thing working. *(Jiggles lever and we hear something*
5   *click.)* Ah, that does it. Ready?
6   MAN: I'm ready, already. I've been ready for the past fifteen
7   minutes.
8   LADY: Boy, what a grouch. Hold tight. Here goes! Zoweee!
9   *(She pulls switch, nothing happens.)*
10 MAN: Well?
11 LADY: Nothing happened?
12 MAN: If something happened would I be here in this
13   condition?
14 LADY: Look, fella, this is my first time.
15 MAN: See what happens when they send a woman to do a
16   man's job?
17 LADY: Oh, quiet. Hmmm ... what did I do wrong? Well, don't
18   just sit there.
19 MAN: Try turning the plug around.
20 LADY: Oh, yes ... *(Does some movement behind the chair)* that
21   used to work on the toaster.
22 MAN: Beautiful.
23 LADY: There. Ready?
24 MAN: I'm ready.
25 LADY: Set?
26 MAN: I'm set.
27 LADY: Go! *(She pulls switch. Nothing happens.)*
28 MAN: I'm still here.
29 LADY: Oh ... I feel so foolish.
30 MAN: *(Being understanding)* Look, it's nothing to worry about.
31   *(He turns and looks at her, she is choking back a tear.)* Aw,
32   come on. I hate to see a woman cry.
33 LADY: But if it fails four times, I have to let you go free and
34   then they'll fire me.
35 MAN: Fire you? Isn't this a civil service appointment?

1	LADY:	Yes, but there's a merit clause written in.
2	MAN:	Settle down and take another whack at it.
3	LADY:	Maybe it's your cap. Do you have a bobby pin?
4	MAN:	No, they took them away from me in my cell.
5	LADY:	While I'm fixing this, you want to see the chaplain?
6	MAN:	Naw, I've already straightened him out. Well, all right,
7		send him in. What the heck.
8	LADY:	I'll call him. Now, where would he be? *(Looks off.)* Oh,
9		there he is — taking up a collection.
10	MAN:	*(Looks off in same direction.)* Boy, these things sure pull
11		in crowds, don't they?
12	LADY:	Well, you had good media coverage, good air time,
13		heavy ink.
14	MAN:	Those tabloids always sensationalize. I'm just a run-
15		of-the-mill murderer.
16	LADY:	Go on. You had lots of things going for you that made
17		your case interesting.
18	MAN:	I don't really think so . . .
19	LADY:	You're just being modest. That won't get you
20		anywhere in life. Ah . . . there it is. OK, hold on, here we
21		go again.
22	MAN:	I'm ready . . . again.
23	LADY:	*(Pulls switch — nothing.)* Oh, nuts!
24	MAN:	Oh, for heaven's sake.
25	LADY:	Stop whining.
26	MAN:	I don't want to harp . . .
27	LADY:	Then don't.
28	MAN:	*(After a pause, he turns to look at her closely.)* Hey, look.
29		Let's be friends. I want to ask you something.
30	LADY:	Ask.
31	MAN:	What's a sweet kid like you doing in a place like this?
32	LADY:	A girl has to make a living.
33	MAN:	Sure, but to compromise your moral beliefs?
34	LADY:	What do you mean by that?
35	MAN:	Look, you're intelligent, right?

1   LADY: Most people think so.
2   MAN: A liberal free-thinker?
3   LADY: Sure.
4   MAN: You believe in charity, aid to the poor, free education,
5   the right of every citizen to speak out?
6   LADY: Sure.
7   MAN: You're against capital punishment?
8   LADY: Of course!
9   MAN: Well, this is capital punishment.
10 LADY: *(Puzzled)* What is?
11 MAN: This. What you're doing. Pulling the switch, taking a
12   human life.
13 LADY: It is?
14 MAN: Of course.
15 LADY: I thought capital punishment had something to do
16   with money.
17 MAN: El wrongo. It's taking another life, baby. The hot seat,
18   the long corridor, the old pit, the long haul . . .
19 LADY: Oh, how grim.
20 MAN: *(Continuing in somber tones)* . . . the deep six . . . the
21   darkness dirge . . . the dirt nap . . .
22 LADY: *(Convinced)* Oh, I feel awful. *(Determined)* In that case,
23   I'm backing out. I'll fail once more on purpose. That will
24   make it four times and you'll go free.
25 MAN: *(He made it; smiles happily.)* Sweet liberal, understanding
26   baby mine. You're a humanitarian. Fake it once and
27   unstrap me.
28 LADY: Righto.
29 MAN: When they tell you there's no decency left in this man's
30   world, turn the other ear.
31 LADY: You're a liberal too, aren't you?
32 MAN: Through and through.
33 LADY: Against capital punishment?
34 MAN: You know it. Come on, let's get going with the old fake
35   switcherooney.

1	LADY:	Then why did you kill that man?
2	MAN:	I had a reason. He tried to steal my collection of hand-
3		carved walnuts.
4	LADY:	*(Very serious)* Doesn't seem like much of a reason.
5	MAN:	Best reason in the world. Think about it. What say,
6		let's get on with it, huh? *(Starts to wiggle out of straps.)*
7	LADY:	I mean, you kill someone, you've got to have a reason. A
8		good reason.
9	MAN:	No lectures, huh? Let's move.
10	LADY:	I've changed my mind.
11	MAN:	*(Feels it slipping away)* You what?
12	LADY:	Changed my mind. You're not so liberal and
13		understanding after all.
14	MAN:	Hey, no value judgments. Set me free.
15	LADY:	I don't think so.
16	MAN:	*(Making a pitch)* Look, you're young, pretty, bright. I'm
17		about your age. Come on, let me go. We can make
18		beautiful music together.
19	LADY:	Sorry, fraud. I hate hypocrisy more than anything.
20	MAN:	I'm no hypocrite. Murderer yes, hypocrite no.
21	LADY:	You're a phony. Here goes. *(Moves toward switch.)*
22	MAN:	*(Resigned)* Well, I gave it my best shot.
23	LADY:	*(Hand on switch)* More power to you! *(She pauses, looks*
24		*at man as he looks up at her. Doubt shows on her face as the*
25		*stage goes dark.)*
26	ANNOUNCER:	*(Comes out as lights come up. He addresses*
27		*audience.)* Well, did she or didn't she? Did she do her job
28		or let the man go free? *(He can listen to audience and make*
29		*a spot decision based on the volume for each side, or he can ask*
39		*for a show of hands for each point of view. If announcer believes*
31		*that the majority said she didn't pull the switch, he says:)*
32	ANNOUNCER:	*(Continued)* And aren't we glad she didn't pull
33		the switch? Say hello to our stars. *(He introduces them.)*
34		*(If the audience votes that she did pull the switch)*
35	ANNOUNCER:	*(Continued)* Well, you feel she *did* pull the

1	switch. No doubt a difficult decision. And we thank you
2	for participating in our exercise. And how about
3	thanking the performers who presented our minidrama.
4	*(Brings out MAN and LADY after announcing them. They bow*
5	*until curtain, or lights go out.)*
6	
7	
8	
9	
10	
11	
12	
13	
14	
15	
16	
17	
18	
19	
20	
21	
22	
23	
24	
25	
26	
27	
28	
29	
30	
31	
32	
33	
34	
35	

#11

Truth in Packaging

CAST: ANNOUNCER, male or female; PAUL Peccancy, president of the Peccancy and Purloin Packagers Incorporated; PRISCILLA Purloin, vice president of the company.

SETTING: Conference table with two chairs. Several packages of cereal, two bowls and a spoon or two are on the table.

ANNOUNCER: **Much has been said about government investigations into the food industry, particularly the packaging of foods. The federal officials call it truth in packaging and say they're protecting the consumer from being ripped off. Packagers, notably the smaller, borderline type, call it government interference aimed at stifling creative marketing.**

Let's look in now at the conference table at this group called Peccancy and Purloin Packagers Incorporated, and the two top officers of their most important committee, the group in charge of Putting Food in Packages in a Highly Deceptive Manner.
(OPENING: We see PAUL Peccancy and PRISCILLA Purloin seated at the table.)

PAUL: Those Fascists down in Washington are investigating us again.

PRISCILLA: Yes, chief. We've got to come up with some sophisticated gimmicks so we can hoodwink the public in peace.

PAUL: Got anything nice? You know, tricky?

PRISCILLA: How about this? We keep the same size jars of applesauce — six and three-quarter ounces, but we change the label to six and seven-eighths?

1   PAUL: So Mrs. Housewive thinks she's getting an extra
2   eighth of an ounce.
3   PRISCILLA: That's a lot of applesauce we save.
4   PAUL: I'm thinking more along the line of a mathematical
5   twister.
6   PRISCILLA: I've been dipping into that area, too. You mean
7   like a pound and fourteen fluid ounces of pineapple juice
8   for fifty-five cents compared with two quarts and two
9   ounces for a dollar fifteen?
10   PAUL: *(Pleased)* That's the ticket! We'll drive those ladies
11   bananas. With those kids pushing and shoving they'll buy
12   two of everything.
13   PRISCILLA: It'll work.
14   PAUL: And why not incorporate some of the updated
15   mathematics mechanisms on the label? Toss in a couple
16   of components, parallel figures, addition factors and
17   reciprocal equalizers.
18   PRISCILLA: Great! And we jazz the package up with
19   forceful symbols in vibrant colors for impulse buying.
20   PAUL: Beautiful. That's money in the bank. What else have
21   you and the gang come up with?
22   PRISCILLA: Oh, the usual half-filled salt boxes, *(Gestures or*
23   *holds up boxes on table)* cereal boxes, soap pad boxes and
24   dog biscuit boxes.
25   PAUL: Those pooches won't be any the wiser. What about
26   labeling to snare the reluctant ones?
27   PRISCILLA: *(Reads from list)* We have large, extra large, super
28   large, super extra large, colossal economy size, super
29   economy size, *(Voice rising with excitement as she reads)*
30   money-saving super extra, large large, extra large,
31   outrageously big and tremendous! *(Pauses, gasping for*
32   *breath.)*
33   PAUL: Your gang is doing great.
34   PRISCILLA: Wait, there's more.
35   PAUL: Go! You're on a roll.

1	PRISCILLA: *(Holds up can of ham.)* **A precooked ham tin in**
2	**the shape of a lovely woman. And . . . it lights up in the**
3	**dark in case the man of the house wants a midnight snack.**
4	PAUL: **It sings! I hear the melody. The cash register concerto.**
5	PRISCILLA: **Glad you like it.**
6	PAUL: **I think we can knock it off for today. You've done well.**
7	PRISCILLA: **Wait. I've saved the best for last.**
8	PAUL: **There's more?**
9	PRISCILLA: *(Holds up package.)* **Nice package, right?**
10	PAUL: *(Acknowledging)* **Nice package. Name brand cereal.**
11	PRISCILLA: **Right. Now watch this.** *(She opens top of box and*
12	*shakes it. Nothing happens. The box is empty.)* **Jumping on**
13	**the fast-food bandwagon, it goes for eighty-nine cents —**
14	**its *pre-eaten food!***
15	PAUL: **Marvelous! Wonderful! You made me happy. Say, let's**
16	**knock it off and I'll take you across to the Steak House**
17	**and buy you a big steak.**
18	PRISCILLA: **You mean** *(Smiling)* **a giant, jumbo, super large,**
19	**extra big, super big, outrageously big and tremendous**
20	**steak?**
21	PAUL: **You got it. Let's go.**
22	PRISCILLA: *(Straightening up her clothes, looking very feminine)*
23	**Let me freshen up.** *(PRISCILLA exits. PAUL watches*
24	*admiringly.)*
25	PAUL: *Now, that's truth in packaging!*
26	
27	
28	
29	
30	
31	
32	
33	
34	
35	

#12

TV 's Johnny Urbane — Intellectual Detective

CAST: ANNOUNCER, male or female, preferably Off-Stage as he
or she has numerous lines near the end of the skit. SALLY,
sexy, stylishly dressed, in her late twenties; JOHNNY Urbane,
confident, well-dressed, articulate.

SETTING: Desk for officer JOHNNY Urbane, set up so he faces
audience. Chair to one side for suspects — in this case, SALLY.

PROPS: Purse, gun, rope, phone, pen, pad.

**ANNOUNCER: TV has brought us numerous detectives who
have become well-known to viewers. We've had Columbo,
McCloud, Barnaby Jones and many more. But none of
these ever could be considered an intellectual officer of
the law. But now we have one — Johnny Urbane,
intellectual detective and knowledgeable lieutenant.
We've been fortunate to have a scene from the pilot film
of the series. So let's look in on Johnny Urbane.**
(OPENING: JOHNNY is at desk, talking into phone.)

JOHNNY: *(With winning smile)* **She may not be a criminal,
sergeant. Maybe merely misdirected. Send her in.** *(Hangs
up phone and awaits the arrival of SALLY, who enters promptly.
She is attractive. JOHNNY is impressed, but he has a job to do.)*
Sit down, miss. *(She sits down on chair near desk. JOHNNY
is sure of himself.)* **Now, miss, don't tell me. Let me tell you.
You stole that purse** *(Gesturing to her bag)* **you're holding
because you are motivated by a drive to make your
husband notice you. You are frustrated, ill-tempered,
neglected. You have kleptomaniacal propensities which
you could no longer stifle. Ergo, you took the purse. Right?**

SALLY: El wrongo, buddy, el wrongo. I *killed* my husband. I

1   kept the gun in this purse. I killed him because *he* was
2   motivated by a drive to make *me* notice *him.* He was
3   frustrated, ill-tempered and neglected, flathead.
4   JOHNNY: The word is flatfoot, if you must use street
5   terminology.
6   SALLY: You're beautiful. You're all wrong. Are you on salary
7   or do you get paid by the blunder?
8   JOHNNY: Please, miss, you're facing a serious charge. Tell
9   me, was your husband over five feet tall?
10   SALLY: Yes. Why?
11   JOHNNY: That's bad. Grand murder. If he was under five
12   feet, it would only be petty murder. Get off with a fine.
13   Let me see the gun. *(She hesitates.)* Come on, I won't keep
14   it. Oh, I get it now. Mistrustful. Unhappy childhood.
15   Father a weirdo. Undependable. You don't know what
16   life expects of you. Unaware of your role in society. Tell
17   Judge Willoughby your story. He'll understand. He's
18   pretty weird himself and he's very lenient with people
19   who don't know what they do and why they do it.
20   SALLY: Here. *(She hands him the gun.)*
21   JOHNNY: Nice gun. What kind?
22   SALLY: Colt forty-five. Marked down from fifty-nine.
23   JOHNNY: This is becoming quite clear. Your husband was a
24   failure in business. He projects his failure by using you
25   as a whipping girl. He heaps calumny upon your fair head,
26   showers you with insults. The judge will understand. His
27   wife does the same thing to him.
28   SALLY: My husband was OK. It's just that I didn't like him
29   playing around.
30   JOHNNY: *(Happily)* Ahah! Cherchez la femme! That's French.
31   Who was the other woman?
32   SALLY: No other woman. Me. He was playing around with
33   me, pal, and I didn't like it.
34   JOHNNY: Ah, I see it now. You're inhibited, undemonstrative,
35   incapable of appreciating and reacting to the normal

1   devotions extended by a loving husband.
2   SALLY: Listen up, Mackie. Playing around . . . games. All the
3   time games. Quoits in the morning. Horseshoes in the
4   afternoon. Bingo at night.
5   JOHNNY: Played bingo and finally his number came up.
6   SALLY: You got that right. The number was B-4 . . . *before* he
7   died, he moaned a lot.
8   JOHNNY: *(Admiringly)* Clever play on words. The judge will
9   like you. He does crossword puzzles with a pen. *(JOHNNY*
10   *leans back in chair and he has a piece of rope in his hands which*
11   *he twirls and ties into a series of knots.)*
12   SALLY: What's with the twine?
13   JOHNNY: Just an intellectual hobby. Decreases tension. I
14   spell out ancient Egyptian letterings and decipher them.
15   Heightens my mental agility. You may have it if you wish.
16   It might occupy you during your period of confinement.
17   SALLY: *(Takes rope.)* I'll treasure every knot.
18   JOHNNY: Think nothing of it.
19   SALLY: That's about the size of it. *(She rises and exits.)*
20   ANNOUNCER: *(Off-Stage)* As the lovely widow heads for
21   trial, our illustrious egghead keeps busy solving cases.
22   *(JOHNNY gets on phone and mouths silent words. Rifles through*
23   *papers, makes notes on pad.)* He solved the case of the hard-
24   bitten iron worker who wanted to know who was biting
25   him so hard.
26   He performed emergency surgery on a nubile Persian
27   princess who was trapped in an automatic flower vending
28   machine — he removed her inhibitions.
29   But each day, Lieutenant Johnny Urbane waited
30   anxiously to hear about the fate of the lovely widow. She
31   was his favorite case. He had used all his big words on her.
32   Finally . . . *(Phone rings. JOHNNY grabs it and talks into*
33   *it.)*
34   JOHNNY: Intellectual Detective Urbane here.
35   ANNOUNCER: *(Possibly different voice Off-Stage)* The case of the

1   lovely widow is over, Urbane. Hung jury.

2   JOHNNY: Hung hury?

3   ANNOUNCER: *(Off-Stage)* Yeah. She hung the jury, one by

4   one. And she used a hunk of twisted rope some stupid

5   lunkhead gave her. *(Stunned, JOHNNY puts down phone,*

6   *slumps back in chair. Then he brightens. Picks up phone.)*

7   JOHNNY: *(Into phone)* Mabel, bring me an encyclopedia,

8   a dictionary, five books on psychology, Roget's Thesaurus,

9   Dick Tracy's Book on Crime Solving Made Easy. And get

10   me the phone number of the lovely widow. Toy with me,

11   eh? She'll learn what it means to trick . . . *(Stentorian voice*

12   *as he sits up straight.)* Johnny Urbane, intellectual

13   detective, knowledgeable lieutenant and erudite

14   investigator!

15

16

17

18

19

20

21

22

23

24

25

26

27

28

29

30

31

32

33

34

35

#13

TV or Not TV? — That Is the Question

CAST: ANNOUNCER, male or female, On-Stage or Off; JERRY, the husband, a man in his forties; LILLIAN, his wife, approximately the same age.

SETTING: Living room. Chairs, telephone, TV set or large box with back toward audience, simulating a TV set.

ANNOUNCER: Recently a team of sociologists offered a typical family a cash prize and a week-long vacation in Bermuda if they didn't watch television for a full week. Nice offer, but could the average American family refrain from TV for seven full days? Could you? Let's see what happens when Jerry and Lillian take a shot at winning some money and an all-expense paid vacation by abstaining from watching the tube.
(OPENING: Stage is empty. JERRY walks in, gazes at the blank TV set and nervously sits down in a chair opposite it. LILLIAN comes in and sits in a chair across the way.)
LILLIAN: Don't you dare turn on that set, Jerry. I've never been to Bermuda.
JERRY: What's so great about Bermuda? I'd just as soon go to Fargo, North Dakota.
LILLIAN: Fargo, North Dakota? What have they got there?
JERRY: Television for one thing.
LILLIAN: Now stop talking like that. Only one more day to go and we get that money and the trip.
JERRY: Money, money, money. Everybody thinks of money. What about enjoying life?
LILLIAN: We'll enjoy it more with money on a cruise to Bermuda.

1   **JERRY:** *(Disgruntled)* **Yeah, yeah.**

2   ***SOUND EFFECT:*** Phone rings. LILLIAN answers it.

3   **LILLIAN:** *(Calling to JERRY)* **Don't you go near that TV.**

4   **JERRY: Yeah, yeah.**

5   **LILLIAN:** *(Into phone)* **Hello? Oh, hi, Mabel.** *(JERRY gets up*

6   *and starts pacing back and forth. LILLIAN keeps a watchful eye*

7   *on him.)* **No fooling? What color? Purple. How much? Well,**

8   **I must say the price is right.**

9   **JERRY: Price is Right!** *(Starts toward TV.)*

10   **LILLIAN: Jerry . . .** *(Gives him hard look; he sits down. Into phone)*

11   **Really? Well, you know that sibling rivalry business.**

12   **Guess it's just another family feud.**

13   **JERRY: Family Feud!** *(Starts for TV.)*

14   **LILLIAN:** *(Warning him)* **Sit down, Jerry.** *(He does so, reluctantly.*

15   *Into phone)* **Well, it's hard to take sides. Guess she's just**

16   **wrestling with her conscience.**

17   **JERRY: Wrestling. Saturday night wrestling! Midgets from**

18   **the Orient. Sumo wrestlers from Japan!** *(He looks at*

19   *LILLIAN and slumps back into his chair.)*

20   **LILLIAN:** *(Into phone)* **Really? Nothing serious I hope. Where?**

21   **Medical Center?**

22   **JERRY: Medical Center?** *(Grabs stomach.)* **I'm getting sick!**

23   *(He starts toward TV, but LILLIAN has her eye on him.)*

24   **LILLIAN: Sit down. You're not sick. And they've got that set**

25   **monitored. Don't touch it! I want to see Bermuda!** *(He sits*

26   *back down and she resumes her conversation.)* **He always has**

27   **his sense of humor. Right. He finds a laugh in everything.**

28   **JERRY: Laugh-In?** *(Looks at LILLIAN and sits back in chair.)*

29   **LILLIAN:** *(Into phone)* **No fooling? The bank said that? That**

30   **puts the whole deal in jeopardy.**

31   **JERRY: Jeopardy?! Alex Trebek! What is this happening**

32   **to me for?**

33   **LILLIAN:** *(Into phone)* **She did? Wow! That's a lot of money.**

34   **She really hit the jackpot.**

35   **JERRY: Jackpot! Will you get off that phone?!**

1   **LILLIAN:**   *(Shushes him and continues talking.)* **Right. Well, they**
2   **say if you wait long enough you'll strike it rich.**
3   **JERRY:**   **Strike it Rich!** *(Starts for the TV set.)*
4   **LILLIAN:**   *(Shouting at him)* **Sit down! Where's your self-**
5   **control?**
6   **JERRY:**   *(Automatically)* **Self-control!** *(Stops and thinks.)* **No,**
7   **that's no show. What am I getting excited about that for?**
8   *(He slumps back into chair.)*
9 ‹ **LILLIAN:**   *(Into phone)* **Yes, I heard that. The boy is a real**
10   **terror. She calls him a young Frankenstein!**
11   **JERRY:**   **Young Frankenstein! Starring Gene Wilder, Peter**
12   **Boyle and Marty Feldman.** *(Starts toward TV set. She points*
13   *her finger at him and he sits back down.)*
14   **LILLIAN:**   *(To JERRY)* **I want to see Bermuda! Just a while**
15   **longer.**
16   **JERRY:**   *(Disgruntled)* **Yeah, yeah.**
17   **LILLIAN:**   *(Into phone)* **Hmmm . . . Well, maybe we can make it**
18   **then. What night? Monday night?** *(JERRY leaps from his*
19   *seat, snaps on the set, watches it and then kicks in the TV set.)*
20   **JERRY:**   **Monday Night Football!** *(Looks at watch.)* **We made it!**
21   **Bermuda, here we come!**
22   **LILLIAN:**   **No we didn't. You peeked at the set. No Bermuda.**
23   **JERRY:**   **No Bermuda?**
24   **LILLIAN:**   *(Sympathetically)* **No . . . but you tried your best,**
25   **Jerry.**
26   **JERRY:**   **Yeah, but I blew it.**
27   **LILLIAN:**   *(She embraces him.)* **Well, they say Fargo, North**
28   **Dakota is nice this time of year.** *(They embrace at curtain*
29   *or blackout.)*
30
31
32
33
34
35

#14

Boy Meets Girl Between Floors

CAST: VOICE, male or female, male preferred, Off-Stage; BOY, mid-20's, likeable, friendly; GIRL, mid-20's, pretty, pleasant.

NOTE: We need the VOICE Off-Stage during the entire sketch. For the musical interludes, recorded music would be best, but the VOICE could sing the few bars required.

VOICE: **Our world is becoming increasingly machine and computer oriented. Yes, we are programmed into a high tech society. Cars talk to us, computer games speak out with instructions, but sometimes things go wrong. Witness.** *(Sound of elevator music)*
(Stage is empty. BOY enters from one side and stands in a vacant area which becomes an elevator. He turns and faces audience. GIRL comes in from other side and moves to the same area. She turns and they are standing next to each other, both facing the audience. A bank of buttons is located at one side of the elevator. If a real frame for the elevator and a simulated array of buttons could be provided it would help. If not, both can be imaginary.)

BOY: *(To GIRL)* **Floor?**

GIRL: *(Eyes him, noting they are alone in the elevator.)* **Forty-eight.** *(BOY pushes button. We note, by their actions, that the elevator door closes.)*

BOY: **Too rich for my blood. I only go to forty-five.**

GIRL: *(Nods)* **Good.**

BOY: *(Noticing GIRL is pretty, decides he wants to know her. He tries the old line.)* **Come here often?**

GIRL: *(A quick look)* **I work here.**

BOY: **Good for you. I'm looking for a job.**

GIRL: *(Looks him over.)* **Good luck.**

1　BOY:　It's in marketing.

2　GIRL:　That's nice.

3　BOY:　What do you do?

4　GIRL:　Administrative assistant.

5　BOY:　Sounds important.

6　GIRL:　Oh ... not really. *(The two of them simultaneously give a*

7　　　　*little start. They are trapped in the elevator. She says with more*

8　　　　*than a little apprehension.)* **We're stuck!**

9　BOY:　*(Looks up to where floor guide would be.)* **Between thirty-**

10　　　　**three and thirty-four.** *(Trying to be cool, gives her a big smile.)*

11　　　　**This time we almost made it, didn't we, girl ...** *(He can*

12　　　　*sing it, if desired.)*

13　GIRL:　*(Ignoring him)* **Isn't there an emergency bell?**

14　BOY:　**There must be in that huge collection.** *(Gesturing to*

15　　　　*buttons)*

16　GIRL:　**Well, push one.**

17　BOY:　**Ladies first.**

18　GIRL:　*(A little stiffly)* **You don't have to let me go first because**

19　　　　**I'm a lady.**

20　BOY:　*(With deep bow)* **I did it because I'm a gentleman.**

21　GIRL:　**I certainly hope so.**

22　BOY:　*(Looks up and around.)* **The music stopped.**

23　GIRL:　**Not important.**

24　BOY:　**I love the Carioca.** *(Waltz, tango, rhumba, whatever was*

25　　　　*playing.)*

26　GIRL:　**Here goes.** *(Pushes button.)*

27　VOICE:　*(Stentorian, if male; authoritarian if female.)* **Thank you**

28　　　　**for shopping Main Street Music. All credit cards**

29　　　　**accepted.** *(Both are surprised and a little alarmed. Music*

30　　　　*resumes.)*

31　BOY:　*(Recovering quickly and smiling)* **I can name that tune in**

32　　　　**three notes.**

33　GIRL:　**Something's wrong.**

34　BOY:　**You pushed the wrong button.**

35　GIRL:　**You can do better? Try.** *(Gestures toward buttons.)*

1	BOY:	*(Clowning, puts a hand over one eye.)* **Eenie, meenie, minie,**
2		**moe, Larry and Curley. My mother told me to choose this**
3		**here one.** *(He pushes.)*
4	VOICE:	**It's 10 o'clock. Do you know where your guidance**
5		**counselor is?**
6	BOY:	*(To buttons)* **Aw, come on!**
7	GIRL:	**You see a counselor?**
8	BOY:	**It's a machine. Don't listen to it.**
9	GIRL:	*(Relieved)* **Oh . . . then nothing's wrong. At least you're**
10		**wise enough to seek help.**
11	BOY:	**I don't need help.**
12	GIRL:	**Most people go through the denial stage until they hit**
13	.	**rock bottom.**
14	BOY:	**We'll both hit rock bottom if this thing falls.**
15	GIRL:	*(Chastened)* **I'll push a button.** *(Does so.)*
16	VOICE:	**Your three minutes are up. Please deposit twenty-**
17		**five cents for overtime.** *(Automatically the BOY reaches into*
18		*his pocket and comes up dry.)*
19	BOY:	**You got a quarter?**
20	GIRL:	*(Mimicking BOY)* **It's only a machine. Don't listen to it.**
21	BOY:	**Just thinking of you. When that phone company gets**
22		**on your case . . .**
23	GIRL:	**Your turn.** *(Gestures toward buttons.)* **Do better.** *(BOY*
24		*smiling confidently, does so.)*
25	VOICE:	**Please fasten your safety belts.**
26	BOY:	**That's it. We're gonna drop!**
27	VOICE:	*(Sings)* **"How deep is the ocean . . ."** *(GIRL shrieks and*
28		*clings to BOY, who enjoys it and regains his composure.)*
29	BOY:	*(Softly, soothingly, holding her close)* **There, there . . .**
30	GIRL:	*(Pulls away.)* **You did that on purpose!**
31	BOY:	**How could I know? It's only a machine. Don't listen to it.**
32	GIRL:	**Keep away from that. I'll try it.** *(GIRL pushes button.)*
33	VOICE:	*(Nasally)* **At the tone, the time will be exactly 9:15.**
34		*(Tone sounds.)*
35	BOY:	*(Smiling, moving close to girl)* **That gives us plenty of time**

1   to get acquainted.

2   GIRL: *(Having none of it)* **Keep away.** *(Reaches for button.)*

3   BOY: **Hey, it's my turn.**

4   GIRL: **Oh, OK, but be careful.**

5   BOY: *(Big smile)* **As long as we're together ... just you and**

6   **me.** *(Pushes button.)*

7   VOICE: **That line is out of order.**

8   BOY: *(Reacting)* **Just a joke. Only kidding.**

9   GIRL: **You shouldn't joke about things like that.**

10   BOY: **Like what?**

11   GIRL: **You know ... together.**

12   BOY: **Just trying to ease the tension ... a little levity.**

13   GIRL: **Yes ... I see.**

14   BOY: **Your turn.** *(GIRL pushes button.)*

15   VOICE: *(Official sounding)* **The countdown begins ... ten ...**

16   **nine ... eight ... seven ...**

17   BOY: *(Shouting)* **We're blasting off!** *(GIRL shrieks and clings to*

18   *him again. BOY smiles.)* **There, there — as long as we're**

19   **together.** *(Puts arm around her.)*

20   GIRL: *(Pulling away)* **You said it was only a joke. Push the**

21   **button.** *(BOY pushes button.)*

22   VOICE: **Do not fold, staple or mutilate.**

23   BOY: *(Angrily)* **Aw, come on, fella.** *(Lady)*

24   GIRL: **Listen to him.** *(Her)*

25   BOY: **It's only a machine. Don't listen to it.**

26   GIRL: **My turn.** *(Pushes button. We hear the Charleston. BOY and*

27   *GIRL, by reflex, both start dancing the Charleston. Music stops*

28   *and they stop dancing, looking at each other sheepishly.)*

29   BOY: **Say, you're pretty good.**

30   GIRL: **So are you.**

31   BOY: **Well, I try to keep up with the latest.**

32   GIRL: **You know, this isn't getting us out of here.**

33   BOY: **Right. Here goes.** *(Pushes button.)*

34   VOICE: *(Unctuously if male, seductively if female.)* **Lonely? Need**

35   **companionship? Just call me at 1-800-555-5555 ... anytime.**

1	Day or night. Only twenty-six dollars for the first minute
2	and nineteen dollars a minute thereafter. I'll be waiting.
3	
4	*(If voice was female, BOY whips out pen and pad.)*
5	BOY: What was that number?
6	GIRL: It's only a machine. Don't listen to it.
7	*(If male voice, eliminate above two lines.)*
8	
9	GIRL: Boy, there are some sick people out there. Imagine.
10	BOY: Don't worry about it. Too many sickos around to worry
11	about them all. Go ahead. It's your turn.
12	GIRL: You go ahead. I'll sit this one out. *(Gazes at board.)*
13	BOY: OK. *(Pushes button.)*
14	VOICE: Men, are you tired, run-down, feeling washed-out?
15	BOY: *(Irritated)* Why do they always pick on men?
16	GIRL: Oh, don't start whining.
17	BOY: *(Getting steamed)* Could it be because men work harder?
18	Do tougher work, beat their brains out competing in a
19	dog-eat-dog world from morning to night?
20	GIRL: *(After brief pause, coolly)* You don't even have a job.
21	BOY: OK, don't start. I could have a great position if this
22	thing would get moving.
23	GIRL: *(Teasing, not malicious)* Sure, vice president in charge of
24	everything.
25	BOY: Well, you never know.
26	GIRL: Why not take charge of getting us free.
27	BOY: *(Challenged)* I'll do just that. *(Pushes button hard.)*
28	VOICE: *(Sternly)* Uncle Sam wants you! *(BOY snaps to attention*
29	*and salutes smartly.)* Not you! Her!
30	BOY: Aw, come on. *(Slaps rows of buttons.)*
31	GIRL: Stop. Don't anger him. *(Her)* We'll never get out of here.
32	BOY: Well, in that case . . . *(Extends hand.)* My name's Charley.
33	GIRL: *(Accepting it)* Betsy.
34	BOY: Like Betsy Ross? American flag?
35	GIRL: Why not? *(Gestures to buttons.)* Uncle Sam wants me.

1   *(They both laugh and stare at each other in warm, friendly*
2   *fashion.)*
3 **BOY:**   **Why don't you take a shot at it?**
4 **GIRL:**   **OK.** *(Pushes button.)*
5 **VOICE:**   *(Soothing, calm)* **This is your captain speaking. Just**
6   **push button number seven and you will glide in smoothly**
7   **for a perfect landing.** *(GIRL does so. They both give a sudden*
8   *start and relax. They turn to face audience, hold hands and smile*
9   *at each other. They pause, then start out toward audience hand*
10   *in hand. VOICE calls after them.)* **Hope you enjoyed your**
11   **trip. Good luck.** *(Hand in hand, BOY and GIRL exit happily.)*
12   *(NOTE: Romantic music might be helpful here, or maybe a*
13   *spirited few bars of "Off We Go, Into the Wild Blue Yonder.")*
14
15
16
17
18
19
20
21
22
23
24
25
26
27
28
29
30
31
32
33
34
35

#15

Love Life in the South Seas

CAST: OSWALD Brenner is the host of an "intellectual" TV show. He is wearing a conservative suit. Dr. Leona SLUSH, noted student of human behavior, has just returned from a trip to the South Seas. She wears horn-rimmed glasses, a garish explorer's outfit with pith helmet, baggy shorts and blouse, uncomfortable shoes with rolled-down socks. Anything that makes her look dowdy and unattractive can be used. She carries a pointer and wears a large, bulky bag over her shoulder.

SETTING: An interviewer's desk and two chairs. On a stand or rear wall is a map of the general South Pacific area, though it can be substituted for if a genuine one isn't available. It is here we see OSWALD Brenner and Dr. Leona SLUSH seated at the desk.

OSWALD: Well, viewers, by this time you probably have recognized our guest, Doctor Leona Slush . . . *(He's not at all impressed with her looks.)*

SLUSH: *(Interrupting)* **But this is my first TV appearance.**

OSWALD: *(On a roll)* **Well then, you probably haven't recognized her. She's wearing her glasses. Nice rims, Doctor. Well, enough about recognition factors. Let's move right on to the South Seas and the love life therein.**

SLUSH: That's what I'm here for.

OSWALD: I'm sure our audience would be disappointed if you weren't.

SLUSH: Well, whenever we anthropologists discuss love in the South Seas, there is always one point of agreement — it's there. You can learn a lot when you study native customs of people who wear nothing above the waist.

1   Even to picnics.

2   OSWALD: Yes ... well ... *(SLUSH stands up with pointer in*
3   *hand. You can see OSWALD is dismayed by her appearance.*
4   *She lumbers to the map with her bulky bag tossed over her*
5   *shoulder. She adjusts her glasses several times during her talk.)*

6   SLUSH: Our first stop if Pago Grunti, *(Points to spot on map)*
7   a tiny, pelvis-shaped island where there are thirty girls
8   to one boy and the females have no qualms about sharing
9   the much sought-after male.

10   OSWALD: Qualms?

11   SLUSH: If they do have qualms they are sent to the
12   dispensary for penicillin shots.

13   Another interesting place is Crandi Crol, the Pearl
14   of the Goona group. *(Points to another spot.)* I remember
15   my first day on the island. Two or three of the husky
16   young males seemed to avoid me ... *(OSWALD looks at*
17   *audience and shakes his head and grimaces — he can see why*
18   *they would avoid her.)* They tittered uneasily and ducked
19   behind their boolahs — girl friends. But I made the first
20   move toward friendship by teaching them the tango ...
21   *(She does a few awkward steps, causing more expressions of*
22   *anguish from OSWALD, who is torn between tightening up or*
23   *bursting into laughter.)* That broke the ice and we became
24   fast friends. We sociologists know a lot of tricks. We have
25   to if we are to get our jobs done.

26   At Crandi Crol I was invited to a wedding of a nine-
27   year-old girl. *(OSWALD shrugs a "so what" look.)* I know ... I
28   know ... you're all as flabbergasted as I was. But it turned
29   out that the bride was a ninety-six-year-old midget with
30   a flair for the comical. Ha, ha, I ha-haed, the joke was on
31   me. The men all laughed and insisted I dance the tango
32   with each and every one of them. *(She does another very*
33   *awkward few steps as the dismayed OSWALD rubs his eyes in*
34   *disbelief.)*

35   Dancing is a big part in the lives of natives in all

these islands. In Hali, Hilo, for instance, they have an endurance dance. It's the battle of the sexes set to music. One male and one female. *(OSWALD opens his hands in a "that figures" gesture.)* The contest is a marathon of stomping and shaking. *(She goes through some bad stomps and shakes while OSWALD can hardly contain himself. She turns to look over at him and he suddenly straightens up and becomes serious.)* I attended a contest in which the woman won. For a whole month, the males had to do all the chores and wave at passing tourist ships, while the women stayed home and ate bonbons as they read novels from the states.

On the Isle of Vestigial, laughing is vital to romance. Giggles are "love play" as we call it. If a suitor can make a maiden laugh, he becomes her *crenchna* or steady beau. If she refuses to laugh and he registers zilch on the laugh meter, he must marry her. And so amidst gales of laughter, they marry. Soon they have a child. Then the laughing stops. *(OSWALD nods knowingly with a "that makes sense" look.)*

On Poona Poona here, *(Points)* the kidney rather than the heart is considered the symbol of romance. Cards are sent on Valentine's Day showing Cupid with a bow shooting an arrow through a kidney. Which is fine, I guess ... if you like kidneys. *(OSWALD, clowning it up, grins maniacally and rubs his stomach like a kid saying "yum-yum.")*

On Balloney Low there is no word for romance as such. The closest thing is *vemya*, meaning to nuzzle longingly or to flinch.

On Bagi Summi, if a young warrior kills an armadillo, he may propose to any girl on the island. If she accepts, they marry. If she refuses, he is sympathized with and given a job as town librarian, gets free laundry service for a month, and can sleep late Saturday mornings. I've

#16

Killer Company

CAST: ANNOUNCER, male or female, On-Stage or Off; GEORGE, On-Stage; GIL, Off-Stage, phone filter only.

SETTING: Desk and chair. Phone on desk which is used by GEORGE.

ANNOUNCER: Unfortunately, throughout the world today, there are many wars being fought. There's fighting going on in countries you may never have even heard of. When you have this fighting going on you're going to have mercenaries, killers for hire, paid assassins, terrorists for dollars. And they are well-paid too. Naturally, when money's available there's always an agent, manager, middle-man. Men like Gil O-Teen. And there are people who hire killers — at a price. Such a man is George Smith. Let's see how he goes about hiring a paid professional killer to aid his cause. Maybe there might be a lesson here about what could happen to people who take human life too lightly.

GEORGE: *(Into phone)* Gil? George.

GIL: *(Voice filter. He's unseen.)* Hi, Georgie baby.

GEORGE: Guess you know why I'm calling.

GIL: You need somebody.

GEORGE: You heard about Pete getting it.

GIL: Yeah, ain't that a shame? He was one of the great ones. How many kills did he have? Sixty? Sixty-five?

GEORGE: Exactly sixty-eight confirmed and seven probables. Had a fog one day so thick you couldn't see a hand grenade in front of your face, so we lost exact count. Got anybody there ready for the big time?

1	GIL:	George, sweetie, you're calling at a bad time. Most of my
2		top drawer people are either in Africa or the mid-East.
3		So many regimes, so many openings. They're making a
4		pile. It's a killer's market.
5	GEORGE:	Can the sales pitch, Gil. This is old George talking.
6		I'll go high for the right man. And no ordinary firing
7		squad man this time. I'm a light sleeper.
8	GIL:	OK, but no paying me in sugar this time. Last time your
9		drivers were careless about where they dumped it. I had
10		to shovel a path of sugar to get to the garage. Of course,
11		the kids liked it. They built a sugar man in the front yard.
12		Used bullets for eyes and a dagger for his nose. Cutest
13		thing you ever saw.
14	GEORGE:	Don't get saccharine on my money, Gil. This is
15		long distance. Now what kind of executioner can you
16		give me?
17	GIL:	Got a good boy for you, George, young performer named
18		Eddie Slaughter. Been around — Hungary, Korea, Spain.
19		And he'll save you money. You know that last meal bit?
20		Well, Eddie doesn't give them a selection. Either the guy
21		eats stew or else he goes hungry.
22	GEORGE:	I don't want a run-of-the-mill guy. I need someone
23		who makes the big sound, grabs the headlines. We've been
24		run off the front pages lately.
25	GIL:	Got a novelty act you might like. Fellow touches off
26		volcanoes. He'll destroy a whole village for you.
27	GEORGE:	Get with it, Gil. Look at my country — not even
28		one volcano.
29	GIL:	Have you got any bottomless pits? He's great at pits.
30		Those loud screams of guys going down. Sends a message
31		to bystanders — your message.
32	GEORGE:	No pits. Look, I want a guy who looks like George
33		Raft, wears double-breasteds, puts oil in his hair and can
34		do the Cubanola Glide. A guy that looks like a killer.
35	GIL:	I see. Prepare the enemy for what will happen if they

1   don't fall in line.

2   GEORGE: Exactly.

3   GIL: You're asking for the moon, George. No got. Hey, I got a

4   guy that specializes in those slow, lingering deaths. Does

5   the old Chinese torture bit. Straps the victim down on a

6   table and then drops little Chinese fellows on his forehead

7   till the guy goes bananas.

8   GEORGE: *(Impatiently)* Gil, I'm running a country. I have to

9   move fascist ... er ... I mean fast. No slow deaths.

10   GIL: Hey! Got a real wild man. He flies a windmill.

11   GEORGE: The man flies a windmill?

12   GIL: Right. A windmill. Picked it up from a guy in Holland

13   and stuck a souped-up engine in it. Let me tell you when

14   he comes ripping through the streets of town, those big

15   blades whirling, it's something you just don't forget. I

16   mean he's Panicsville. Sometimes he gets some loser on

17   those blades and throws him twenty, thirty miles. He's a

18   real show-stopper.

19   GEORGE: Too noisy. Too undependable. He might accidentally

20   pick up one of my own men. Besides, I may have to give

21   him flight pay.

22   GIL: Well, guess we can't do business today, George. Hey!

23   Hold it. A guy just walked into my office. I know this guy.

24   He's your answer. Does a revival act. Guillotine.

25   GEORGE: Guillotine?

26   GIL: Right. He's socko. A smasheroo. Interested?

27   GEORGE: *(Thinking)* Well, nostalgia is big right now. How

28   much?

29   GIL: Five thousand a week and a percentage.

30   GEORGE: What kind of percentage?

31   GIL: Ten per cent off the top. Ha-ha. Get it? Ten per cent off

32   the top ... guillotine ...

33   GEORGE: No lousy gags at these rates, huh? I'm on long

34   distance. Five thousand is too high. Make it four

35   thousand. I mean I could do it myself.

1	GIL: Don't make an assassin of yourself, George. What say?
2	Five thousand and thirteen solid weeks?
3	GEORGE: OK. Deal.
4	GIL: Great. I'll put him on the plane tonight and you'll have
5	him first thing in the morning. I'll tell him the news. *(To*
6	*guy in office)* Ben, great news. Got you booked in for
7	thirteen with George on the Central American circuit.
8	What's that? You don't like him. No, he's not bad. Don't
9	listen to those guys. George is an all right guy. Hey, take
10	it easy. Back off! *(Alarmed)* What are you doing?! Sit down!
11	Get back there! No . . . no . . . *(Screams — then silence.)*
12	GEORGE: *(Alarmed)* Gil! Gil!
13	GIL: *(GIL's voice as woman operator)* Sorry, your party has been
14	disconnected.
15	
16	
17	
18	
19	
20	
21	
22	
23	
24	
25	
26	
27	
28	
29	
30	
31	
32	
33	
34	
35	

#17

The Wrestling Game — No Holds Barred

CAST: ANNOUNCER, male or female, On-Stage or Off; INTER-
VIEWER, male, typical TV wrestling announcer; Wrestler,
BULK Brogan, male, burly, wrestler type.

SETTING: Interviewing set-up at ringside. Both performers will
stand as there is some motion involved. Anything to heighten
the aura of being ringside would help.

PROPS: ANNOUNCER can hold a hand mike. BULK can be
attired in crazy wrestling get-up as seen on TV, or a plain
leopard skin outfit.

**ANNOUNCER: Wrestling began in ancient times and is with
us today bigger than ever, thanks mainly to television.
There was Greco-Roman grappling, catch-as-catch-can,
and now, anything goes. We have developed a new batch
of wrestling idols — Andre the Giant, Killer Kowalski,
The Mean Machine and the man we have with us tonight,
one of the men fans say will soon wear the champion's
belt, Bulk Brogan.**

**INTERVIEWER: Bulk, welcome to the Splintered Limb Arena,
site of many famous matches.**

BULK: *(Slightly dazed)* Is that where we are? *(Looks around.)*

INTERVIEWER: Well, you travel so much.

BULK: Well, I travel so much.

**INTERVIEWER: You're still on the move up the ladder, but
you've been picking 'em up and flinging 'em down for
some time now. Can you remember your first battle?**

BULK: I can't even remember my *last* battle.

INTERVIEWER: When will you fight again?

BULK: As soon as the swelling goes down.

1	INTERVIEWER: The odds were nine to five on your last
2	match against Leo Lasagna that you would lose. What
3	are the odds for your next fight?
4	BULK: Four to one I don't show up.
5	INTERVIEWER: People like to compare today's wrestlers
6	with the old-timers. Do you think today's Andre the Giant
7	could beat Man Mountain Dean?
8	BULK: Sure . . . if they fought today.
9	INTERVIEWER: What sort of diet do you have to stay in shape?
10	BULK: Every match day I buy six pounds of raw steak. I eat
11	three pounds and save three pounds for my eyes after
12	the fight.
13	INTERVIEWER: A lot of butting goes on out there, I guess.
14	Do you have a trainer to take care of you?
15	BULK: Of course. After each fall I sit back on the stool and my
16	trainer goes to work. I get rubbed down the back, up the
17	spine, over the eyes, behind the ears, under the chin,
18	along my wrists . . .
19	INTERVIEWER: Wait a minute. That doesn't sound right.
20	What's your trainer's name?
21	BULK: Raquel.
22	INTERVIEWER: I see. Speaking of women, Danny "Devil
23	Dog" Dawson used to bring his girl, Brigitte, to training
24	camp with him. Did you ever try that?
25	BULK: I tried it once . . . but Danny got mad.
26	INTERVIEWER: What is your advice to young wrestlers?
27	BULK: Stay low . . . low . . . *(Demonstrates, crouching and*
28	*circling, wrestler-style)* Get as low as possible.
29	INTERVIEWER: So he can't hit you?
30	BULK: So he can't *see* you.
31	INTERVIEWER: Are you a bellicose grappler?
32	BULK: *(Angrily)* I never threw a match in my life!
33	INTERVIEWER: Right. OK. You know, you're a pretty big
34	guy. Why do they have you listed in the program as a
35	middleweight?

1   BULK: I've got all my weight around the middle. *(Pats belly.)*

2   INTERVIEWER: Wrestlers take some pretty hard knocks.
3   You ever been bruised or banged up?

4   BULK: You kidding? I've been body slammed to the canvas
5   so much I got cauliflower hips.

6   INTERVIEWER: Well, you're pretty good at that yourself.
7   The last time you fought Percy Vandermeer, you
8   slammed him down pretty hard. How come they didn't
9   count that a pin and give you the match?

10   BULK: The ref was under him.

11   INTERVIEWER: So Percy's shoulders weren't on the canvas,
12   I see. What are your other famous holds?

13   BULK: On Crusher Caldwell I used the toe hold.

14   INTERVIEWER: That can hurt.

15   BULK: I still got his toe. I keep it in a locket to wear when I
16   go out formally. Wanna see the toe? It's in my foot locker.

17   INTERVIEWER: I'll take a rain check. Any other holds?

18   BULK: I've got the double reverse twist, spin and slam. Here,
19   I'll show it to you. *(Advances toward INTERVIEWER who*
20   *evades him quickly.)*

21   INTERVIEWER: Not me. Calm down. Get a grip on yourself.

22   BULK: Grip on yourself. Hey, that's pretty good.

23   INTERVIEWER: Yes. Any other holds?

24   BULK: Well, I got my famous airplane spin. *(He holds arms*
25   *above head as if holding opponent and spins around in circles.)*

26   INTERVIEWER: Hold it, Bulk. This is Professional Wrestling
27   Spotlight, not American Bandstand.

28   BULK: Sorry.

29   INTERVIEWER: I see the next match is about to begin. Now
30   you've fought some of the roughest wrestlers around —
31   Slippy McBride, Slam Hollister and Two-Ton Terranova.
32   Can you tell me about them?

33   BULK: They are three of the toughest women I ever fought.

34   INTERVIEWER: Thank you, Bulk, and good night fans.

35

#18

Honest Abe — Can He Stay That Way?

CAST: ANNOUNCER, male or female, On-Stage or Off; ABE
Lincoln; MANNIE, his White House aide and political advisor.
He is glib, sure of himself.

SETTING: Table or desk with two chairs.

*(OPENING: Both men are On-Stage. ABE is seated, holding
paper and pencil. MANNIE is seated.)*

ANNOUNCER: Throughout the history of our country, our
presidents have had speech writers and advisors who
suggest ways in which the leaders can grab more votes
and, more importantly, not offend any particular group.
One president, considered by many to be the finest writer
in White House history, did his own work. But could he
withstand today's pressures brought about by powerful
blocs of voters? Let's take a look as we see this president,
Abraham Lincoln, going over a speech with his advisor,
Mannie.

MANNIE: OK, Abe, lay it on me.

ABE: Fourscore and seven years ago our fathers brought . . .

MANNIE: Hold it right there, Abe. Fathers? You just can't
say fathers. Mothers were involved here too.

ABE: I know, but . . .

MANNIE: Do you realize the clout these women's groups
have?

ABE: Women's groups?

MANNIE: They're all over the place. You've got your WAWA's,
your . . .

ABE: *(Puzzled)* WAWA's?

MANNIE: Wide Awake Women of America. You've got MAN . . .

1 **got a picture of an armadillo killer who proposed to me.**
2 **Would you like to see it?** *(OSWALD, in terror tries to slump*
3 *down while shaking his head "no" quite vigorously. SLUSH*
4 *grapples with her bag as she fumbles for some pictures. She*
5 *approaches a wary OSWALD and shoves some pictures at him.*
6 *He reluctantly takes one and looks. He whistles. Surprised, she*
7 *snatches the pictures back from him.)* **Wrong picture. Give**
8 **me that. You're too short to see that.**
9 OSWALD: *(Puzzled)* **Too short?** *(He stares at her.)* **Guess it gets**
10 **pretty hot down there. I mean with that sun beating**
11 **unceasingly down on your skull.**
12 SLUSH: **It gets pretty warm all right, buddy boy.** *(She sits*
13 *down next to him, making him uncomfortable.)* **You know,**
14 **down there as well as all over the world, it's the male**
15 **who pursues the female.** *(She removes her glasses and leans*
16 *over.)* **All over the world except in** *(Name local city or stage).*
17 *(OSWALD's eyes widen as SLUSH takes off her pith helmet,*
18 *shakes out her hair, rubs her hands together. She eyes OSWALD*
19 *and straightens up. OSWALD, fear in his eyes, stands up*
20 *nervously as SLUSH comes closer.)*
21 OSWALD: **Except in** *(Names city or state)*, **that's where the . . .**
22 SLUSH: *(Moving in)* **. . . females chase the males. You got it,**
23 **buddy boy.** *(OSWALD, inching slowly off, addresses audience.)*
24 OSWALD: **Same time, same place, next week, audience.** *(His*
25 *eyes widen as SLUSH advances.)* **I hope!** *(With that he turns*
26 *and races off with SLUSH in hot pursuit.)*
27
28
29
30
31
32
33
34
35

TWO MEN

1	ABE: *(Interrupting)* Man? Thought you said women's groups.
2	MANNIE: It is a women's group . . . a mean, militant mob.
3	MAN is the acronym for Mean and Nasty.
4	ABE: Look, Mannie . . .
5	MANNIE: You've got the DAR.
6	ABE: The Daughters I know.
7	MANNIE: There's the WASHUS, the . . .
8	ABE: Washus? The Indians have always liked me . . .
9	MANNIE: Not Indians, Abe. Women. WASHUS stands for
10	Women Against Sexual Harassment from Union Soldiers.
11	ABE: Sexual harassment by soldiers? Never. At least no Union
12	soldiers.
13	MANNIE: Well, I've seen some of them and I can't believe
14	anybody would *want* to harass them. I'm with you on that
15	one, Abe, but they're a force you have to consider.
16	ABE: OK, I'm considering.
17	MANNIE: Let's go back. Instead of fathers . . . substitute
18	parents.
19	ABE: *(Checking speech)* Hmm . . . fourscore and seven years
20	ago our parents brought forth . . . I don't know . . . doesn't
21	have the same zing.
22	MANNIE: Zing, schming, it don't mean a thing if you ain't
23	got that swing with the female voters.
24	ABE: *(Reluctantly)* Gee, I don't know . . .
25	MANNIE: You can't say fathers.
26	ABE: What about freedom of speech, the first amendment?
27	MANNIE: Hey, you can't hide behind the constitution. You're
28	the president.
29	ABE: I'm a citizen and I'm entitled to my civil rights.
30	MANNIE: Civil rights? You ain't no minority.
31	ABE: No minority? How many guys do you know that are six-
32	feet-four, have a beard and wear a stovepipe hat?
33	MANNIE: Yeah, I want to talk to you about that hat later.
34	But let's get back to your little talk here.
35	ABE: *(Irritated, hands the speech over to MANNIE.)* Here, you

1   read it. *(MANNIE takes paper.)*

2   MANNIE: Yeah, I'll have a look-see. Maybe I can punch it up.

3   ABE: *(Stands, talks story-telling style.)* **A fellow came up to me**

4   **the other day and asked, "Mr. President, how long should**

5   **a man's legs be?"**

6   MANNIE: *(Looking up)* **"Just long enough to reach the**

7   **ground." Hey, we heard it. Don't run it into the ground.**

8   **Let me finish this.**

9   ABE: *(Chastened, sits back down.)* **OK, OK.**

10   MANNIE: Not bad, not bad. I go along with all this until we

11   get to this — *(Reads aloud)* "that this nation, under God . . ."

12   Abe. *(Shakes head.)* Abey baby. What are you doing to me?

13   You can't say "under God."

14   ABE: And why not?

15   MANNIE: Do you realize how many God-fearing atheists and

16   agnostics you got out there?

17   ABE: Isn't that an oxymoron or am I missing something?

18   MANNIE: I don't care how intelligent they are. They vote,

19   that's all I know.

20   ABE: And I want "under God" in there, that's all I know.

21   MANNIE: Look, these people are tough. They got groups.

22   And believe me, these atheists got lots of friends in

23   Congress.

24   ABE: *That* I can believe.

25   MANNIE: I mean you've got your ALAB — Atheists Living

26   and Breathing. The Triple A, Agnostic Atheist

27   Association . . . see, they'll combine to gang up on you.

28   And one of the biggest — the Atheists Society In the

29   Northern Interior and the New Earth — or ASININE.

30   ABE: You got *that* right.

31   MANNIE: You can't hurt atheists, Abe. Once they pull that

32   curtain shut in the booth, they vote with their hearts and

33   souls.

34   ABE: Let me tell you a little story . . .

35   MANNIE: This isn't going to be one of those aphorisms like the

1   one about McClellan having his headquarters where his
2   hindquarters should be?
3 ABE: *(Going right on)* **This atheist died and he's lying there in**
4   **his coffin. And my Aunt Polly said: "Look at him. All**
5   **dressed up and no place to go."**
6 MANNIE: Yeah, right Abe. Tell Aunt Polly she gets a three on
7   the laugh meter.
8 ABE: I like "under God." And it'll catch on. I bet someday
9   we'll have a saying something like "in God we trust" on
10   all our money.
11 MANNIE: Yeah. And the moon is made of green liederkranz
12   and it don't rain in Indianapolis in the summertime.
13   *(MANNIE hands the paper back.)* **Here, make those two**
14   **changes.** *(ABE refuses, stands up.)*
15 ABE: Keep it. Print it. It stands as it is. No president should
16   ever succumb to the pressures of the power-seeking, self-
17   serving organizations, no matter what kind. This is a
18   government "of the people, by the people, for the
19   people" — read that — *(Gesturing to paper)* it's in there.
20   That means *all* the *people*, not big lobbies and angry
21   mobs. *(ABE exits.)*
22 MANNIE: *(Resigned to defeat, shrugs and glances at paper.*
23   *Murmurs as he reads.)* **Gettysburg address. Address?** *(Calls*
24   *after ABE.)* **Abe, call this an address? You ain't got no**
25   **street or number!** *(Shouts even louder.)* **And you forgot the**
26   **zip code!** *(Starts after ABE, then returns and sits down, shakes*
27   *head.)* **I don't know what I'm gonna do with that boy.**
28
29
30
31
32
33
34
35

#19

The House of Incision Is at Hand

CAST: ANNOUNCER, male or female, On-Stage or Off; Broadcasters, HOWARD and FRANK.

SETTING: Broadcasters' table with two mikes and some papers and pens.

ANNOUNCER: It's true, Monday Night Football is television's number one ratings grabber each week. But competition looms. With all the medical shows getting fine ratings — St. Elsewhere, Quincy, General Hospital, Medical Center and reruns of Marcus Welby, Ben Casey, Dr. Kildare — viewers undoubtedly are hooked on medical programs. Why not combine the two? Why not "Monday Night Surgery?" Let's look and listen.

(OPENING: FRANK and HOWARD are seated behind the table, facing toward audience.)

FRANK: Good evening, surgery fans. Welcome to "Monday Night Surgery." Tonight's presentation is coming to you live from under the lights of the operating arena in New York's Metropolitan Hospital, which moved recently to the New Jersey Meadowlands.

HOWARD: We're speaking to you from table-side and, believe me when I tell you, folks, that you feel the electric currents of tension running through this standing-room-only crowd jam-packed into this modern facility for the long-awaited appendectomy playoffs.

FRANK: This match-up has been sold out for weeks. Rumors have it that scalpers were getting two hundred dollars a ticket.

HOWARD: We'll be watching two of the best in the game. Big

1   Bill Cannady from Wilmington, Delaware, against Sam
2   "The Slicer" Sensabaugh, the wily scalpel-wielder from
3   Secaucus, New Jersey.
4 FRANK: Big Bill was known as Mr. Inside back at Johns
5   Hopkins. He's strong and cool and powerful. Now Sam
6   the Slicer is a slit-and-slash type of a cutter. He won't
7   overpower you, but he's a cutey and he's got more moves
8   than a belly dancer with a strange rash.
9 HOWARD: As in all playoffs, the competitors will play
10   separate courses.
11 FRANK: Right. Big Bill will operate on Arlie "Fat Henry"
12   Grickle, a 300-pound dental technician who is being
13   wheeled in now by the pretty miniskirted nurses here at
14   Metropolitan.
15 HOWARD: Grickle is some formidable set-up. Look at those
16   hazards and traps. I'd say this is about a par four
17   appendectomy.
18 FRANK: Exactly right. Here comes 280-pound Jim Whoopsner,
19   registered chorus boy, who will be worked on by Sam
20   Sensabaugh. The crowd comes alive now as Doctor
21   Cannady sharpens his scalpel and Sam warms up by
22   flexing his fingers in that peculiar way of his — running
23   them lengthwise across the face of an intern.
24 HOWARD: And they're just about ready. It's axiomatic in
25   play-for-pay medicine that the doctor who gets off to a
26   good start with a straight fairway incision has a
27   psychological advantage, forcing his opponent to play
28   catch-up surgery. Here's Big Bill ready to tee off.
29 FRANK: He waggles the scalpel, goes into that picture
30   backswing and ... right down the fairway, landing
31   maybe a quarter-inch away from the peritoneum.
32 HOWARD: Fine field position. Here's Sam, the hometown
33   favorite, using that curious interlocking grip on his
34   scalpel.
35 FRANK: Nice shot by Sam. Not as far as Big Bill's first blast,

1   but it's right on the fairway.

2   HOWARD: You'll notice Sam uses a big scalpel for his size.

3   That's about a nine-inch, eight-ouncer. But he'll cut down

4   to a shorter, lighter scalpel when the weather gets warmer

5   and the season drags on. You knew him in college, didn't

6   you, Frank?

7   FRANK: No.

8   HOWARD: *(Going right on)* You future surgeons out there,

9   note the intensity with which Sam approaches his shot.

10   Hope you noticed that. He came here to operate.

11   FRANK: Here's Big Bill. *(Pause)* Beautiful! Right on the crest

12   of the peritoneum, within easy putting distance.

13   HOWARD: I love Sam's intensity as he lines up his second

14   shot. Look at the knotted muscles in his jaw, the

15   unblinking eyes, the throbbing vein in his forehead . . .

16   FRANK: I think he has a cramp, Howard.

17   HOWARD: There's Sam's second move. *(Pause)* A soft angle

18   shot, just missing the ascending colon on the left. Now,

19   a brief pause before returning to "Monday Night Surgery."

20   FRANK: Fans, as you might know, I was a varsity medical

21   man in college, but Howard here had to learn all about

22   the game right from the basics. Great job, Howard.

23   HOWARD: I think so. When I first started I thought a terminal

24   case was a piece of luggage at a railroad station. But I've

25   learned and I must say it's inspiring to be associated with

26   a man of your caliber, Frank.

27   FRANK: How's that, Howard?

28   HOWARD: Well, fans, you will remember last Friday a man

29   gave his kidney to a woman; yesterday you will recall

30   another man gave his left lung to a boy, and just this

31   morning on the crosstown bus, Frank gave his seat to a lady.

32   FRANK: Thank you, Howard. Any gentleman would have

33   done the same. Now back to live action. The crowd is really

34   into it now. Big Bill holds up his hand for quiet. They're

35   still noisy. Big Bill steps away.

HOWARD: *(Starts to lecture.)* I sometimes questions the basic integrity of surgery fans. Rooting at your home hospital, you owe a visiting doctor the courtesy and respect of any visiting professional . . .

FRANK: Ah . . . there he goes. Beauty! He's got it! He snared the appendix with a birdie three. The crowd is very silent now.

HOWARD: Believe me when I tell you, fans, it's vital that fair play be an essential ingredient, not only in this business, but in the fabric of our very society . . .

FRANK: The crowd is roaring now for Sam as he moves into position.

HOWARD: Of course, you have to go to the top. The behavior of the owners is not impeccable. The recruiting, the crassness of the moguls, the covert manipulations in awarding scholarships, the blatant seduction of promising interns, the under-the-operating-table payoffs to outstanding rookies . . .

FRANK: Sam shoots. Oh . . . rough luck. He shanked it. Big Bill wins! That means twenty thousand dollars and a gold basin, symbolic of the championship.

HOWARD: *(Still lecturing)* . . . the despoliation, the bargaining for bodies has to have an effect on interns finding their way through their tender, formative years. The heinous practice of convincing all-around doctors, general practitioners, to switch to surgery is reprehensible. Frank, what do you think of proselytizing?

FRANK: Well, if it involves two consenting adults . . .

HOWARD: *(Taken aback)* Yes . . . well . . . OK . . . tune in next week, fans, when we will bring to you live from the Hollywood Bowl the final round of the "Plastic Surgery Playoffs."

FRANK: Top doctors working on famous movie stars will smooth wrinkles, tighten jowls, soften crow's feet, straighten noses, remove blemishes and who knows what all.

1   HOWARD: So tune in next week for "New Faces of 1990."
2   FRANK: Thank you and good night.
3
4
5
6
7
8
9
10
11
12
13
14
15
16
17
18
19
20
21
22
23
24
25
26
27
28
29
30
31
32
33
34
35

#20

Sending Away for Those Magazine Offers

CAST: ANNOUNCER, male or female, On-Stage or Off; JIM and
STAN. They are good friends, both casual and likeable.

SETTING: A table where the two performers can sit, or they can do
their duolog standing.

PROPS: Magazine or two and a newspaper to refer to when
discussing the ads.

ANNOUNCER: How many of us have sent away for those
intriguing ads in newspapers and magazines? You know,
"Learn Meat Cutting at Home" and "Run down? Cranky?
Grouchy? Send away for a year's supply of our vitamins
you can take anytime, anywhere." Or words to that effect.
These inducements are guaranteed to make you rich . . . or
popular . . . or intelligent . . . or healthy . . . or all four. But
do they work? Are they completely honest? Let's see.
*(OPENING: JIM is standing or sitting alone On-Stage, reading
a newspaper. STAN enters.)*
STAN: *(Greeting him cheerfully)* Hey, old buddy, haven't you
finished the comics yet?
JIM: Oh, yeah. Just that these ads are . . . I don't know . . .
guess they're just not for me.
STAN: Back to those ads again, eh? What is it this time?
JIM: *(Reads)* "Send now for this new plan to develop muscles
and become stronger."
STAN: And?
JIM: I sent away . . . couldn't open the envelope.
STAN: *(Sympathizing)* Yeah, they stick 'em tight these days. So,
it's not bad being weak. *(Squeezes JIM's bicep.)*
JIM: Yeah, and I sent away for a course in developing a push-

1   button memory.

2   STAN: *(Straight man)* **A push-button memory. What went**
3   **wrong?**

4   JIM: **I sent twenty-seven dollars for the course, now I can't**
5   **remember where I put it.**

6   STAN: **We all forget things.**

7   JIM: **Look at these.** *(Holds paper over and they both look at it. Reads.)*
8   **"Learn karate! Attack your friends without warning!"**

9   STAN: **That won't win you any *new* friends.**

10   JIM: *(Reads)* **"Be popular!"**

11   STAN: **Well, maybe I was wrong.**

12   JIM: *(Reads)* **"Learn to throw your voice."**

13   STAN: **In the comfort of your own living room?**

14   JIM: **No, anywhere, I guess. Here's one. "Learn to hypnotize!"**

15   STAN: *(Looks at ad.)* **Hey, pretty girl coming right at you.** *(Closes*
16   *eyes and holds arms out as if sleepwalking.)*

17   JIM: **Looks interesting.**

18   STAN: *(Looking at paper again)* **She is a knockout. And look at**
19   **the gown she's almost wearing.**

20   JIM: *(Reads)* **"Dance your way into her heart. Be popular! Do**
21   **the rhumba, tango and all the latest steps. Tiptoe your**
22   **way into her good graces."**

23   STAN: **Something to check out.**

24   JIM: **I did. That's when I began to think my mailman was**
25   **opening my mail.**

26   STAN: **Oh?**

27   JIM: **Yeah, he's booked for five shows on American Bandstand.**

28   STAN: **I noticed him outside. Does a mean boogaloo.**

29   JIM: **Look at this.** *(STAN looks; JIM reads.)* **"Discover the**
30   **world of art. Women from all over the world posing for**
31   **the top brush wielders extant."**

32   STAN: *(Questioning)* **Extant?**

33   JIM: **That's what it says.**

34   STAN: *(Looks)* **It does indeed. Send for any?**

35   JIM: **Thought about it, then I figured no because there wouldn't**

1   be any redeeming social value.
2   STAN: Right. You wouldn't want to get in trouble with the
3   authorities. Did you answer any ad at all?
4   JIM: Yes ... I'm a little ashamed. A dating organization.
5   STAN: One of those places that try to get you a date with a
6   girl that fits your likes and tastes.
7   JIM: Right. I wrote and told them I'd be interested in meeting
8   a tall blonde with a great personality, a glamorous
9   lifestyle and a wonderful walk.
10 STAN: And?
11 JIM: They sent me a picture, address and phone number of
12   Sven, a six-feet-four-inch lifeguard at Atlantic City.
13 STAN: Those ads can be deceiving. I don't know ... guess
14   they're all out to nail you, make some money.
15 JIM: Yeah, but they do work once in a while.
16 STAN: I never heard of any of the ads that worked.
17 JIM: Well, my cousin took a body-building course through
18   the mail.
19 STAN: I've seen the ads. This worked?
20 JIM: Worked great. In three months — a body like Arnold
21   Schwartzenegger.
22 STAN: Wonderful.
23 JIM: Yeah, but her husband got so jealous of her physique he
24   walked out and hasn't come back.
25 STAN: Well, win some, lose some.
26 JIM: Right. See ya around. *(Turns and starts off.)*
27 STAN: Take care. *(Goes off in other direction.)*
28
29
30
31
32
33
34
35

#21

Cookie Conway — Culture Consultant

CAST: ANNOUNCER, male or female, On-Stage or Off; TOM, the interviewer; COOKIE, culture consultant, a fey character.

SETTING: Table or desk with two chairs. TV interview set-up.

ANNOUNCER: **Right now the country is in the midst of the biggest cultural boom in history. People are wrapped up in painting, off-beat movies, sculpture, poetry, drama, music and every other form of an artist's freedom of expression. But there are some people who don't really have a grasp on this swing to culture. If someone calls some painter an impressionist, do you feel he's talking about Rich Little? If you feel left out in the cold when the conversation switches from detergents to drama, or baseball to ballet, then this program will help. We bring you Cookie Conway, Culture Consultant.**

(OPENING: TOM is dressed in normal, everyday attire. He is seated. COOKIE comes in with hair plastered down, ascot doubled under his chin and stylish sports jacket. He comports himself with the arrogant assurance that only a thorough knowledge of culture can bring — in some circles.)

TOM: **Good evening, Mr. Conway.**

COOKIE: **Please call me Cookie. My friends love it and I do too.**

TOM: **Right, Cookie.** *(Holds up some papers.)* **I have here a few questions from your audience. Shall we have a go at it?**

COOKIE: **Start it going. No use keeping these culture seekers in the dark.**

TOM: *(Reads)* **"Dear Cookie: Friends tell me the new play by North Carolina Roberts, 'Don't Kiss Me When I'm Angry and I Won't Tell the Truth About You' is very sophisticated.**

1   Is this play sophisticated?"
2 COOKIE: Not really. Actually it's rather a shopworn, stale
3   story of boy finds wart hog, boy loses wart hog, boy gets
4   wart hog.
5 TOM: *(Reads)* "Dear Cookie: I am sick and tired of the
6   conventional ways of painting. Are there any new
7   modern ways of painting?"
8 COOKIE: Yes, *indeedee.* There are some fascinating new
9   ways of expression in painting if the prosaic methods
10   don't tickle your palette. *(Giggles at his play on words.)* For
11   instance, Leonard Gedarby achieved critical acclaim by
12   throwing ink-stained darts into a soiled babushka worn
13   by his wife twenty feet away.
14 TOM: That's unique to say the least.
15 COOKIE: *(Rankled)* And I hope you will. And if Leonard
16   couldn't sell his work to a gallery, he'd peddle them to
17   psychiatrists as Rorschach tests.
18 TOM: Anyone else?
19 COOKIE: Well, you might prefer the method of Skippy
20   Whoopsner. What Skippy does is to dribble tomato soup
21   through his beard into an alabaster bowl.
22 TOM: I've never seen any of his creations.
23 COOKIE: Some of his best works are on exhibition at the
24   Board of Health.
25 TOM: *(Reads)* "Dear Cookie: Could you tell me how many men
26   are in the all-male Russian ballet."
27 COOKIE: Oh, I'd say about half of them.
28 TOM: *(Reads)* "Dear Cookie: I want to be a singer and for my
29   birthday, my boy friend gave me a pair of opera-length
30   hose. How can I tell if they are genuine?
31 COOKIE: Genuine opera-length hose come all the way up to
32   the "Rigoletto."
33 TOM: And that's a nice aria. *(COOKIE gives TOM an irritated
34   glance. TOM continues.)* "Dear Cookie: I'm of Albanian-
35   Norwegian extraction. Do you know many musicians of

1	the same persuasion?"
2	COOKIE: The name of Horescue Detesque, the great drinking
3	glass player comes to mind. Horescue filled drinking
4	glasses with Gatorade and played upon them with
5	chicken legs. He had a three-octave range and created
6	many brilliant works. But a sad fate befell him. Always
7	shy and sensitive, Horescue had a nervous breakdown
8	just before his American debut at Carnegie Hall.
9	TOM: I didn't know that.
10	COOKIE: Well, listen up and I'll proceed. Horescue was so
11	upset he ate his mallets and drank his act.
12	TOM: And today?
13	COOKIE: Today Horescue is living quietly as a wicket
14	mechanic for a team of dancing croquet players.
15	TOM: *(Reads)* "I read recently, Cookie, that you can take any
16	three notes and turn them into a singable melody. Could
17	you do that with these three notes — B and F sharp and
18	A flat."
19	COOKIE: Certainly. What were those three notes again?
20	TOM: B and F sharp and A flat.
21	COOKIE: Sing them for me, will you please? *(TOM sings any*
22	*three notes as COOKIE listens intently. Then he nods head*
23	*confidently. He's got it. He hums the same three notes, as if*
24	*practicing.)* **Here goes.** *(COOKIE sings the three notes, drawing*
25	*them out for full effect, then goes swingingly into "Jingle Bells.")*
26	TOM: Wow! *(Applauds)* **Amazing. A singable melody from just**
27	three notes.
28	COOKIE: It's a gift. I can do it in the comfort of my own living
29	room — and often do.
30	TOM: *(Reads)* "I think Lancelot Lerdoo is the greatest song
31	writer of all time. Agree?"
32	COOKIE: What you probably don't know is that Lancelot
33	Lerdoo did not write those songs he is credited with.
34	Lancelot had a big fat crow come in and whistle for him
35	and he would copy down the melodies note for note. If the

1	crow refused to whistle, Lancelot would threaten it
2	because the crow still had relatives living in the
3	Okefenokee Swamp.
4	TOM: *(Reads)* "Dear Cookie: The great Persian poet, Rama
5	Prurient, recently wrote a third verse to his epic poem
6	'Kanada, Kanada Boom!' Would you recite it please?"
7	COOKIE: No.
8	TOM: *(Reads)* "Dear Cookie: The other night at a cultural
9	kaffee klatsch we talked opera. Someone mentioned
10	'Goose Bumps on Broadway.' Would you outline the story
11	for me?"
12	COOKIE: Happy to. As the name implies, "Goose Bumps on
13	Broadway" is about a professional skydiver who thinks
14	he's smart. He strolls into a forest during a severe storm
15	and is struck by a bolt of cloth hurled by an itinerant
16	muffin taster. Skydiver is stunned, makes a wrong turn
17	at the Philharmonic and, very tired now, falls asleep in
18	an accordion.
19	TOM: In an accordion?
20	COOKIE: *(Irritated)* An accordion. You know...*(Plays*
21	*imaginary accordion)* a stomach Steinway. He suffers
22	serious injury when the accordionist comes out and takes
23	four hot choruses of "Lady of Spain."
24	TOM: Ah, a tragedy.
25	COOKIE: Nope, things lighten up when he falls in love with a
26	pleated woman who later gives birth to a Japanese fan.
27	TOM: Lovely story. *(Shakes head, looks skyward.)* Next letter.
28	*(Reads)* "I understand the great sculptor, Andy Schnick,
29	was critically injured when the plaster dinosaur he was
30	riding split mysteriously in midair at the Museum of
31	Natural Naturalism. Is he still on the critical list?"
32	COOKIE: His name has been removed from the critical list
33	— he died.
34	TOM: *(Reads)* "Dear Cookie: I am a spry sexagenarian and I
35	am appalled at the emphasis on teen-age singing groups

1	and their trashy music. Aren't there any mature musical
2	groups around?"
3	COOKIE: You bet there are. My favorite is the "Golden Age
4	Gangsters." Their big hits include "Put Down Your
5	Crutches and Dance with Me" and "Do You Know Arthur?
6	Arthur Who? Arthur-itis. Yes, I Do." It's on the Geriatrics
7	label.
8	TOM: *(Reads)* "In your opinion, who was the greatest ballet
9	dancer of all time?"
10	COOKIE: Without a doubt it was the late, great Knocky
11	Bagatelle. Knocky always danced outdoors because there
12	was no ceiling high enough for him to dance under. He
13	leaped so high when he came down his slippers were out
14	of style.
15	TOM: No fooling?
16	COOKIE: When it comes to ballet and fashion, I never lie. So
17	one day, Knocky was performing his favorite — the
18	entrechat dix.
19	TOM: And that is?
20	COOKIE: That is where the dancer leaps high in the air, doing
21	rapid pirouettes while crossing and uncrossing his feet.
22	He could spin seven times a second, or seventy complete
23	revolutions on a ten-second flight. And on his greatest —
24	and final leap — he did ninety-eight complete spins.
25	TOM: While crossing and uncrossing his feet?
26	COOKIE: Exactly. Unfortunately, as he neared earth, he
27	couldn't get his feet uncrossed, and spinning rapidly, he
28	twisted himself fourteen feet into the ground.
29	TOM: What a way to go!
30	COOKIE: Well, he died with his slippers on.
31	TOM: Well, that's about it for now, folks. Cookie, do you have
32	your culture tip of the week for your viewers?
33	COOKIE: All you culture fans out there, I strongly suggest
34	you visit the drama festival at the Sunshine Golden Glow
35	Nudist Colony in Quick Glance, Missouri. They have a

whole new concept of presenting Shakespeare called Theater-in-the-Nude. First production is — "As You Like It."

This is Cookie Conway saying "It's nice to be a bird of paradise, but it's better to be a vulture for culture." *(Blows kiss.)* **Love you all.**

About That Ad You Had in the Paper . . .

CAST: ANNOUNCER, male or female, On-Stage or Off; ED Spencer, personnel director at Ballard Industries, about forty-five; JIM Barnstable, the applicant, about thirty-five.

SETTING: Job interview set-up. Desk, with necessary accoutrements and chair for applicant.

ANNOUNCER: The job situation has always been rough for the job seeker, no matter what level he's trying for. Whether it's starting at the bottom, middle management or high level, it's not an easy task, filling out forms, waiting anxiously for a call to set up an appointment, and finally — the interview itself.
(OPENING: ED Spencer is seated at his desk. JIM Barnstable walks in.)

ED: *(Checking paper and greeting JIM)* **Jim Barnstable?**

JIM: Right.

ED: *(Gesturing)* **Sit down.** *(JIM does so. ED goes through some papers.)* **You've had a varied background.**

JIM: Different kinds of experience in the business world. Right.

ED: That's good, because this is a job with a lot of variety. You'll write brochures, make marketing proposals, write and make speeches and in general be an assistant to the big boss and sort of an all-around troubleshooter.

JIM: I've done a little bit of all of those.

ED: Fine. Now I must warn you, Ed, the Big Guy has a few hang-ups, particularly about language in speech and print, and in promptness.

JIM: I can understand that.

1 ED: Do you use offensive language or resort to slang?
2 JIM: Never. I figure my vocalberry is expensive enough so I
3   can commute with my fellow denizens without denigrating
4   the language.
5 ED: *(Thoroughly taken aback. He looks at JIM questioningly.)* **Uh**
6   ... yes ... right. The Big Guy is a stickler for grammar.
7   How's your punctuation?
8 JIM: Never been late a day in my life.
9 ED: No ... I mean ... moving right along. Now you know we
10   deal in medical fields, music, social issues, etcetera. We
11   have a great number of clients.
12 JIM: I'm pretty averse in all of those. I did PR work for a
13   hospital and got plenty of good ink for its expansive care
14   unit. We came out like roses even during an outbreak of
15   eczema. I tell you, it reached epidermis proportions.
16 ED: I see.
17 JIM: And I was buddy-buddy with old Doc Greevely, the
18   head sturgeon.
19 ED: I've heard of him.
20 JIM: Nice guy. Thoughtful. Always deep in the throes of
21   medication. Not one of those medics who go jumping to
22   contusions.
23 ED: Sounds interesting.
24 JIM: I got him front page coverage when he gave the movie
25   actress, Lana Bevel, mouth-to-mouth restitution.
26 ED: Was that a set-up?
27 JIM: No, no. It happened on the splurge of the moment.
28 ED: You just happened to be there.
29 JIM: Right. Johnny on the spotlight.
30 ED: Thought you didn't use slang.
31 JIM: Sorry. That slipped out.
32 ED: The boss hates slang.
33 JIM: Won't happen again, I can insure you.
34 ED: Fine. *(Actually getting used to JIM's lauguage)* **Now about**
35   crime. One of the Big Guy's pet topics.

1	JIM:	I covered the city beat for the Chicago Evening Trans-
2		gression. Used to have long serious concussions with the
3		warden of the big house.
4	ED:	Slang?
5	JIM:	I mean the penitentiary. Sorry. He was the man in
6		charge of the electric chair, in charge of all elocutions.
7	ED:	And how do you feel about capital punishment?
8	JIM:	I think it's a strong detergent against crime.
9	ED:	Right. Do you like pets? The Big Guy loves dogs.
10	JIM:	Oh, yes. I've got a dog. Big dog. One of those mastoids.
11		Very often you can find me and Amos strutting down the
12		main thoroughbred of town.
13	ED:	We do lots of work in the music field. Know music?
14	JIM:	Know it and love it. I relax by going to symphonic
15		concerts. I love the reed section, especially listening to
16		the buffoons. They really wail.
17	ED:	Slang?
18	JIM:	*(Snaps fingers.)* **Oh . . .** *(Catches himself)* **heavenly days!**
19	ED:	OK, Jim, if you'll sit there a minute, I'll run this through
20		our personnel department computer. Be right back.
21	JIM:	**Right.** *(ED takes papers Off-Stage. JIM sits and waits*
22		*anxiously. ED returns. He is smiling. He goes to JIM, who stands*
23		*up.)*
24	ED:	*(Extending hand)* **You're now a member of Ballard**
25		**Industries. Welcome aboard!**
26	JIM:	I got it?
27	ED:	You bet.
28	JIM:	Crazy! You dig?
29	ED:	I'm hip!
30	JIM:	You're my main man.
31	ED:	Groovy. Catch you Monday in the early bright.
32	JIM:	Cool.
33	ED:	Wear some heavy threads.
34	JIM:	*Au reet.* **Hit me five!** *(They give each other the high five as*
35		*JIM starts off.)*

1	ED: You splitting?
2	JIM: Got to shuffle. Plant you now, dig you later.
3	ED: But no slang.
4	JIM: No slang! *(They face each other from across the stage and give*
5	*each other the quick clenched fist victory punch. JIM exits and*
6	*ED sits back down in his chair, shrugs and has that look of a*
7	*confused man. Blackout or curtain.)*
8	
9	
10	
11	
12	
13	
14	
15	
16	
17	
18	
19	
20	
21	
22	
23	
24	
25	
26	
27	
28	
29	
30	
31	
32	
33	
34	
35	

2

3 # The High School Reunion — Number 40

4

5

6 *CAST:*   ANNOUNCER, male or female, On-Stage or Off; ED
7   Morgan; JIM Brant. Both are in their late fifties. They went to
8   high school together and are attending their fortieth high school
9   reunion.

10

11 *SETTING:*   Table with punch bowl and ladle, and a couple of cups.
12   Men do their talking while standing, having met at the punch
13   bowl.

14

15 **ANNOUNCER: High school reunions are a way of life in**
16   **America. Some are joyous occasions, some are a little**
17   **sad. Let's see what happens when Ed Morgan and Jim**
18   **Brant meet at their fortieth high school reunion.**
19   *(OPENING: ED Morgan is standing alone at the punch bowl.*
20   *He dips in and helps himself to a cup of punch. He surveys the*
21   *audience, representing other attendees of the reunion. Soon he*
22   *is joined by JIM Brant. He looks at him.)*

23 **ED: Jim? Jim Brant?**

24 **JIM:**   *(Acknowledging)* **Ed Morgan?**

25 **ED: Right. Football?**

26 **JIM: Swimming.** *(They shake hands convivially.)*

27 **ED: You haven't changed a bit.**

28 **JIM: I've met six other liars who said the same thing.**

29 **ED: A few more pounds maybe.**

30 **JIM: A few less hairs for sure.**

31 **ED: What's it been since the last time?**

32 **JIM: Gee . . . twenty years? Yeah, the twentieth was the last**
33   **time I showed up.**

34 **ED: Me too. That must have been it.**

35 **JIM: Crowds keep getting smaller.**

1	ED:	Lots of people moved away.

1   ED: Lots of people moved away.

2   JIM: And died.

3   ED: That's the grim part.

4   JIM: You still in financing?

5   ED: Yeah. Stocks and bonds.

6   JIM: If I remember you, it was stocks and *blondes.*

7   ED: No more. Married. Settled down. You still in insurance?

8   JIM: Yeah. Like they say, there's no one with endurance like
9   the man who sells insurance. We get you all in the end.

10   ED: I remember that song.

11   JIM: See anybody you recognize?

12   ED: Edna Neville. Now she is one who hasn't changed.

13   JIM: Same weight as she was in high school.

14   ED: *(Laughing)* Yeah ... three hundred eight pounds. *(They*
15   *both laugh and dip into the punch.)*

16   JIM: See Jerry Bettancourt?

17   ED: No ... he died.

18   JIM: Guess that's why he didn't show up. *(They laugh, a little*
19   *hollowly.)*

20   ED: I did see Eloise Hellman.

21   JIM: *(Confirming)* The cheerleader.

22   ED: She never met a football team she didn't like.

23   JIM: Right.

24   ED: She's here alone. The football team couldn't make it.
25   *(They laugh.)*

26   JIM: Hey, how about Penny Finley. Remember her? Wild
27   one. A real terror. Ever hear about her?

28   ED: Sure. She's my wife.

29   JIM: *(Taken aback briefly)* Oh ... yes ... I think I heard that.
30   Any young terrors ... children?

31   ED: Three. Penny's over there. *(Gestures)*

32   JIM: Right. *(Looks over.)*

33   ED: You get married?

34   JIM: Yeah. A little late. Betty couldn't make it. The old
35   arthritis.

1	ED:	Kids?
2	JIM:	Three. Same as you.
3	ED:	It's funny. My oldest is twenty-six. When he was nine I
4		figured he'd win the Nobel Peace Prize. Now we say,
5		"Well, at least he doesn't steal."
6	JIM:	As long as they're healthy.
7	ED:	You know who's not here is Gerry Brenner.
8	JIM:	Gerry was a funny guy.
9	ED:	He was indeed. Some guys are short, some guys are fat,
10		but Gerry was funny.
11	JIM:	Remember he stole the lawn mower and etched a
12		picture of the principal's wife on the lawn?
13	ED:	And added her measurements?
14	JIM:	Oh, yeah. She was a beauty contest winner.
15	ED:	The next year he came back and changed the numbers.
16	JIM:	Yeah. He raised the figures appropriately.
17	ED:	Gerry was a funny guy. Ever heard anything about him?
18	JIM:	No. Let's ask around. *(They dip into the punch bowl and are*
19		*quiet for a second or two.)*
20	ED:	Hey ... great talking to you, Jim. *(Looking off)* Penny's
21		signaling me.
22	JIM:	Right. *(They shake hands.)* Take care of yourself. *(JIM is*
23		*alone and muses aloud as he watches ED leave.)* Boy, I don't
24		know about going to any more of these reunions. Like
25		seeing Frank Donaldson. He changed so much he didn't
26		even recognize me. And everybody else ... *(Looks around*
27		*thoughtfully)* all you get are a bunch of old people who
28		claim they went to school with you. *(He dips into the punch*
29		*bowl, pours himself a cup and sips. Pensively.)* Somehow the
30		old punch is gone.
31		
32		
33		
34		
35		

#24

Religion with the Big Beat

CAST: ANNOUNCER, male or female, On-Stage or Off; PARSON
Carson, a cool musician who is maestro of his flock; JOHN
James, a soon-to-be member of PARSON Carson's parish.

SETTING: Can be open stage, though chairs or a sofa can be used.
PARSON Carson should be carrying an instrument of some
kind. If the performer actually can play it, the effect would be
helpful, getting off a few licks during the conversation.

**ANNOUNCER: You may have read recently of the clarinet-
playing** *(Or other instrument)* **preacher who brings music
to the people he visits, mainly the poor in the southern
part of the country. He's doing great work to help his
people, bringing joy and music to them. But music has
always been an integral part of religion. We've always
had organs and, lately, guitars to add to the religious
services. Let's see what could happen if music were
carried a step farther, making it the big reason for a
particular congregation.**
*(OPENING: PARSON Carson, dressed in cool, but tasteful,
fashion, is On-Stage alone, either playing his instrument or
checking it out. JOHN James comes in. He is rather shy,
diffident.)*
PARSON: *(Eyeing JOHN)* **Greetings, my son. Enter.**
JOHN: Parson Carson?
PARSON: You hit that note right on the head.
**JOHN: I'm very much interested in joining your church,
Parson.**
**PARSON: Crazy.   What   do   you   play?   Horn?   Guitar?
Glockenspiel?**

1   JOHN: I'm not musically inclined.
2   PARSON: Not even the tambourine or ocarina? *(Looks*
3   *skyward.)* **Man, how do you expect to get to heaven?**
4   JOHN: I have a nice sense of rhythm. *(Snaps fingers.)*
5   PARSON: *(Hesitatingly)* Well . . . but man, you ain't gonna
6   please the lead horn man Gabriel. How do you expect to
7   swing in that big Aragon ballroom in the sky?
8   JOHN: Is music all that important?
9   PARSON: First came the lyric . . . then came the beat. Then
10   we tie the package, nice and neat.
11   JOHN: I like it.
12   PARSON: Music is with us all on our way to glory.
13   Why we got one cat who plays lute, flute and drums to
14   boot.
15   JOHN: He's devout.
16   PARSON: Last week he put strings on the collection basket
17   and gave us four choruses of "When the Red, Red Robin
18   Comes Bob, Bob, Bobbin' Along." He's the greatest.
19   JOHN: Everyone has to play?
20   PARSON: Not really. Some of my sextons don't play. They
21   just sit with me during services and fake it. The musicians
22   local says we have to seat two sextons during the sermon
23   even though they don't blow a note.
24   JOHN: Regarding sermons — does your church offer any
25   injunctions to heighten the will power?
26   PARSON: Naw. That's old-time religion. I'm not knockin' it,
27   but character development ain't our province. Of course,
28   when things get groovy, we sometimes repent at the coda,
29   grieve at the bridge and commiserate at the double bar.
30   JOHN: What sort of services do you conduct?
31   PARSON: We ad-lib the sermons, gate. Then later we tub-
32   thump with a beat that's great.
33   JOHN: What are the tenets of your faith?
34   PARSON: We embrace a bit of everything. No real strictures
35   to tighten you up. Keep loose, keep cool, cat. Oh, yeah!

1   JOHN: Well . . . I'd like to give it a try.
2   PARSON: And-a-one, and-a-two and a-welcome to the herd,
3   hipster.
4   JOHN: Thank you. Do I call you padre . . . parson . . . minister?
5   PARSON: Nonsense, brother, just call me maestro. *(He puts*
6   *arm around JOHN and they head off slowly.)* **You see, what**
7   **really matters is that we hit the right note with our fellow**
8   **humans. We all march to a different beat, but in the end**
9   **the joyous melody is the same.**
10   JOHN: *(Enthusiastic now)* **I can dig that!** *(PARSON leads him*
11   *off.)*
12   PARSON: Come on, we're just in time for a guest sermon by
13   the Four Sky Pilots. *(They exit.)*
14
15
16
17
18
19
20
21
22
23
24
25
26
27
28
29
30
31
32
33
34
35

#25

Who's a Loser?

6   *CAST:*   ANNOUNCER, male or female, On-Stage or Off; WALLY
7   and WILLY, both likeable fellows doing their own program on
8   sociology.

10   *SETTING:*   Desk, two chairs, notebooks to read from if the players
11   choose, and a telephone.

ANNOUNCER: One of the more popular one-word descriptives today is that of "loser." If a person fails at something or falls short in his attempts to succeed, he is branded a "loser." But is that fair? If a person doesn't make it, should he be called a "loser?" To find out, let's listen now to two winners, Wally and Willy, to find out just what a loser is.

WALLY: Thank you, Whipsnerd.

WILLY: That person is *not* a loser.

WALLY: The name is, but not the person.

WILLY: Right. Let's get into this situation to clear the whole thing up. Give the public an example of a loser.

WALLY: A loser is a Hindu snake charmer with a deaf cobra.

WILLY: Agreed. That's a loser. Here's one. A loser is a fat flamenco dancer in a condemned building.

WALLY: That qualifies. And so does — a loser is a gigolo with chapped lips.

WILLY: Like it! A loser is a guy who gets a blowout in the spare tire in his trunk.

WALLY: A loser is a pilot who presses the ejector seat button in his helicopter.

WILLY: A loser is a strolling violinist in a waterfront saloon.

WALLY: A loser is a fat tourist who falls asleep at a luau with an apple in his mouth.

1	WILLY:	That's a top drawer loser. Another loser is a piano
2		player in a marching band.
3	WALLY:	Another one is a sailor who gets a battleship tattooed
4		on his chest — and it sinks.
5	WILLY:	A loser is a guy who doesn't know how to give mouth-
6		to-mouth resuscitation without getting emotionally
7		involved.
8	WALLY:	A loser is a six-day bike rider with a five-day
9		deodorant.
10	WILLY:	A loser is an Indian scout with squeaky moccasins.
11	WALLY:	Right. Well, I think that should clear things up for
12		our listeners.
13	WILLY:	I think so. Now they know who the real losers are
14		and they'll be nicer to people who try and just don't make it.
15	WALLY:	Like us. I mean we're not big-time, but you can't call
16		us losers.
17	WILLY:	Certainly not.
18	WALLY:	Ah, here's another one. A loser is a motorist who
19		sticks out his hand for a left turn and whacks a cop right
20		in the mouth.
21	WILLY:	That's a real loser. *(Phone rings; WILLY picks it up.)* **Yes?**
22		**The police? Yes? Wally's here.** *(Listens, nods and hangs up*
23		*phone.)* **The police are on their way over. They want to**
24		**thank you for confessing about whacking the policeman**
25		**right in the mouth.**
26	WALLY:	*(Shakes his head.)* **Me and my big mouth. Just an**
27		**accident.**
28	WILLY:	Sorry, Wally. But you know what that makes you?
29	WALLY:	*(Nodding glumly)* **Right. I'm a loser. A real loser. But**
30		**how about you?**
31	WILLY:	What about me?
32	WALLY:	Remember a while back? You sent away for your
33		family tree and they sent you back a bunch of bananas.
34		You know what that makes you?
35	WILLY:	Right. A loser.

```
1    WALLY:    Well, folks, have to tell you — you've been listening
2             to a couple of . . .
3    WILLY and WALLY:   . . . Losers! Real losers!
4
5
6
7
8
9
10
11
12
13
14
15
16
17
18
19
20
21
22
23
24
25
26
27
28
29
30
31
32
33
34
35
```

#26

Doctor Skullthumper

CAST: ANNOUNCER, male or female, On-Stage or Off; DR. ARBUCKLE, a pleasant, authoritative middle-aged psychiatrist; WILBUR BLAND, the patient, a very shy fellow who is anywhere from twenty-five to fifty.

SETTING: Psychiatrist's office. Desk and chair and any desk appointments deemed necessary by director or performers.

ANNOUNCER: **You know that old saying , "anybody who goes to a psychiatrist should have his head examined." Well, more and more people are having their heads examined all over our land. Is it the stress and strain of daily living? The competitive battling to get ahead? Whatever it is, surveys have shown that one in eight people have some sort of mental or emotional disorder. Seems to me it's more than that. I see offbeat people all the time. Noisy, loud, frightened — or very shy — like this patient.**
(OPENING: DR. ARBUCKLE is seated at his desk, looking at a card or pad. He looks around the room and toward the exit, obviously expecting someone. Then he spots someone Off-Stage.)
ARBUCKLE: *(Calling out)* **Come right in, Mr. Bland.** *(After a few seconds pause, Wilbur BLAND comes out, slowly, with great apprehension. He looks around, sees Dr. ARBUCKLE beckoning him and goes to the desk. He stands before it, looking around the room.)* **Oh . . . no, no couch. Got rid of it. Too many of these patients just lie down and doze off. And when you get a disturbed sumo wrestler snoring on your couch, it's not easy to get him off. I have to call in Nurse Bulkner to haul them away. Sit down, Mr. Bland.** *(BLAND sits down.*

1	*ARBUCKLE reads from card.)* **Wilbur Bland. Shy. Introvert.**
2	**Difficulty speaking in company.**
3	**BLAND:** *(Starts to talk, but can't get words out.)* **I ... I ... uh ...**
4	**uh ...**
5	**ARBUCKLE:** Make that *impossible* to speak in company.
6	How long have you experienced this difficulty?
7	**BLAND:** Uh ... well ... you see ... it was ... *(ARBUCKLE*
8	*sighs and looks at his watch.)*
9	**ARBUCKLE:** Obviously it's a deep-seated problem, but it's
10	not all that rare. Many people are afflicted with this
11	ailment, and believe me, it *is* an ailment despite the fact
12	that some medical men say it's just a device to attract
13	attention. Just relax, Mr. Bland. Nothing to worry about.
14	**BLAND:** Right.
15	**ARBUCKLE:** There you go. I have my own particular cure
16	for this inability to communicate. I call it the Arbuckle
17	Reverse Twist, Give-and-Go Slam Dunk Force. Of course,
18	there are no guarantees for anything in the mind field,
19	but in your case I don't see how it can fail. It requires
20	some effort on your part. Are you willing to try?
21	**BLAND:** *(Nodding)* **Yes, doctor.**
22	**ARBUCKLE:** OK, here's what you do. You provide the impetus
23	from within. All this inability to talk has forced you to
24	sublimate your true feelings. Obviously you have opinions
25	about things and about people. Everybody does. You
26	suppress these thoughts and they build up into a
27	potentially explosive situation and great unhappiness for
28	you. Understand?
29	**BLAND:** *(Nodding)* **Yes.**
30	**ARBUCKLE:** OK. Here's what you do. Did you see all those
31	people out there in my waiting room?
32	**BLAND:** Yes. Lots of them.
33	**ARBUCKLE:** This is the rush season in this field. So I want
34	you to go out there, stand up in front of them, pick out
35	any person that comes into view and tell him or her what

1   you think about them.

2   **BLAND:** *(Pointing to himself)* **Me?**

3   **ARBUCKLE:** **You. Get out there and be perfectly honest and**
4   **forceful.**

5   **BLAND:** **Can I come back to think about what I think about**
6   **them?**

7   **ARBUCKLE:** **No. It has to be from the heart, spontaneous. Do**
8   **it now.**

9   **BLAND: Now?**

10 **ARBUCKLE:** **Now.** *(Forcefully)* **Go!** *(With a start, BLAND gets to*
11 *his feet, hesitates and starts toward audience. He turns and starts*
12 *back, but ARBUCKLE authoritatively shoos him on. BLAND*
13 *gulps and addresses audience, who is now the waiting room*
14 *people. In effect, BLAND will become a Don Rickles-type facing*
15 *a nightclub audience. He summons up his courage and looks out*
16 *at the audience and begins.)*

17 **BLAND:** *(With a good degree of new-found confidence)* **Wow, what**
18 **a group. Looks like there's been a slow leak in a sleazy**
19 **massage parlor.** *(He will aim each jarring remark at an*
20 *individual, real or pretended.)* **Look at that face. Fellow, you**
21 **look like you just won a hundred yard dash in a ninety**
22 **yard gym.**

23   **Hey, lady. Yeah, you. I recognize you. Saw you the**
24 **other day on Main Street wearing a gownless evening strap**
25 **and a pair of glow-in-the-dark hot pants. Is that your**
26 **mother sitting next to you? Ah, yes. Yes, folks, this lady's**
27 **decency, morality and goodness have never been**
28 **questioned . . . in fact, they've never been mentioned.**

29   **And look at that guy. We know about you. This man**
30 **is humble, modest . . . and with good reason.**

31   **Ah, there's a pretty young thing. She never met a**
32 **sumo wrestler she didn't like. But you're OK in my book,**
33 **honey . . . and you know what book** *that* **is.**

34   **There's the university dean. You can talk to him**
35 **about anything — politics, morality, mathematics, world**

1	affairs — he won't understand what you're saying, but
2	you can talk to him.
3	*(Frowns, shudders)* Look at the face on that guy. When
4	he was born the doctor took one look and then slapped
5	his mother instead of him.
6	Hey, look at that guy. Fella ... great face. Anybody
7	else hurt in the accident? I've seen your type before, but
8	not loose.
9	Well, that just about does it. I've had my fun and I
10	know you have too. And if any of you see me on the street,
11	do me a favor — cross over to the other side. *(Very cocky,*
12	*he turns and heads back to ARBUCKLE.)*
13	ARBUCKLE: Marvelous. Great. How do you feel?
14	BLAND: *(Still cocky)* OK. Here he is, folks. The famed
15	psychiatrist, Sigmund Froodcake, founder of the If-You-
16	Can't-Pay-Me-You-Ain't-Crazy School of Medicine.
17	ARBUCKLE: *(Taken aback)* Now wait ...
18	BLAND: *(On a roll)* Treated a schizophrenic and sent him two
19	bills.
20	ARBUCKLE: See here ...
21	BLAND: Great face. When he was born his father passed out
22	cigar butts.
23	ARBUCKLE: Now look ...
24	BLAND: He's willed his brain to science. Science is
25	contesting it.
26	ARBUCKLE: Bland ...
27	BLAND: Doc, if you ever have your life to live over ... live it
28	overseas. *(ARBUCKLE is stunned into open-mouthed silence.*
29	*BLAND looks at him closely.)* When I clap my hands three
30	times, you will awake and won't remember a thing ...
31	ARBUCKLE: *(Recovering)* Now ... I'm warning you ...
32	BLAND: Hey, you've got a ready wit. Let me know when it's
33	ready ... *(With a roar, ARBUCKLE leaps out of his chair at*
34	*BLAND, who, in fear, turns and races out with ARBUCKLE in*
35	*hot pursuit, shouting dire threats at the frightened BLAND.)*

1   **ARBUCKLE:**   **Why you rotten . . .** *(BLAND races out. ARBUCKLE*
2   *halts at the exit line. He turns and returns to his seat. He plops*
3   *down, picks up the card and a pen. He makes a check mark on*
4   *the card. He leans back and smiles with great satisfaction. To*
5   *audience)* **Chalk up another win for old Doc Arbuckle and**
6   **medical science.**
7
8
9
10
11
12
13
14
15
16
17
18
19
20
21
22
23
24
25
26
27
28
29
30
31
32
33
34
35

#27

A Phone Call Plea for Help

CAST: ANNOUNCER, male or female, On-Stage or Off; ABNER
Jones; JOHN Smuckers.

SETTING: Two desks with phones. ABNER is seated at one desk,
JOHN at the other. They will be talking to each other.

**ANNOUNCER: Today's life styles are high tech escapades.
Computers, word processors, a tremendous amount of
multidigit identification numbers for the individual and
his necessary papers can lead to much confusion.
Witness.**

*(ABNER is glancing at sheet of paper he's holding and dialing
phone. It's a long number. He gets through. We hear ring.)*

JOHN: *(Picks up phone.)* **Acme High Life Insurance and Happy
Times Hospitalization.**

ABNER: Hello. I'm a subscriber to your plan and I'd like some
information.

JOHN: Shoot. *(Takes pen and pad.)*

ABNER: I had a little accident *(Looks at index finger of free
hand)* you see . . .

JOHN: Name?

ABNER: I don't know . . . just a small cut on my finger . . . I
don't know what they call it.

JOHN: I mean *your* name.

ABNER: Oh . . . right. Jones. Abner Jones.

JOHN: Abner? Is that with one or two "n's"? *(He writes down
the information he gets from ABNER.)*

ABNER: One.

JOHN: Jones?

ABNER: Right. Just one of the Jones boys. *(Friendly chuckle)*

1	JOHN:	That's nice. Address?
2	ABNER:	3456 Smith Street. Right here in Midville.
3	JOHN:	Zip?
4	ABNER:	What?
5	JOHN:	Your zip code.
6	ABNER:	Oh . . . 55555.
7	JOHN:	Policy number?
8	ABNER:	*(Checking paper)* Have it right here. Policy number is
9		847362-A-8990054-B.
10	JOHN:	You have our A-B policy. That's a good one. Your
11		social security number?
12	ABNER:	Hold it. *(Rifles through wallet.)* Ah . . . *(Reads from card*
13		*he has taken out.)* 990-7890-3121.
14	JOHN:	Driver's license?
15	ABNER:	Oh, yes.
16	JOHN:	Number?
17	ABNER:	Hold it. *(Flips open wallet and reads.)* Number
18		B467210099. Invalid when not wearing corrective lenses.
19	JOHN:	Not important. About your lenses.
20	ABNER:	Right. Just wanted to give you all the information
21		necessary.
22	JOHN:	The firm doesn't care if you wear glasses if you're
23		complaining about your finger.
24	ABNER:	Right. Not necessary.
25	JOHN:	If I wrote down everything you told me, where would
26		I be? I haven't got all day.
27	ABNER:	Look, I don't have all day either. And I'm not
28		complaining about my finger.
29	JOHN:	Sounded like it.
30	ABNER:	I just want to know if I'm covered.
31	JOHN:	Details.
32	ABNER:	What?
33	JOHN:	About your complaint.
34	ABNER:	Right. I was sipping from a can of low-cal grape soda
35		and I . . .

1   JOHN: Low-cal grape . . . *(As he writes)* **Overweight?**

2   ABNER: No . . . I just like low-cal. So I was watching the
3   tube, just dawdling . . .

4   JOHN: Dawdling?

5   ABNER: Dawdling. I dawdle. Everybody dawdles.

6   JOHN: Excessively?

7   ABNER: The normal amount. So I stuck my finger in the top
8   of the can . . .

9   JOHN: *(This strikes him funny and he chokes back a laugh.)* **You**
10   **what?**

11   ABNER: Stuck my finger in the top of the can and . . .

12   JOHN: *(Laughing)* **While dawdling?**

13   ABNER: *(Irritated)* **Yes, while dawdling.**

14   JOHN: *(Not quite choking back a laugh)* **Go on.**

15   ABNER: I'll wait until you finish laughing.

16   JOHN: *(Straightening out)* **Sorry. Go ahead.**

17   ABNER: So I cut my finger. It swelled up. Bled a little. And
18   I'm in a little pain.

19   JOHN: Hurt yourself while dawdling? *(Laughs)*

20   ABNER: Yes! I hurt myself while dawdling!

21   JOHN: *(Laughing)* **Did anybody come over to kiss it and make**
22   **it well?**

23   ABNER: Look, all I want . . . what's your name? For my
24   records, who am I talking to?

25   JOHN: John Smuckers.

26   ABNER: The jelly Smuckers?

27   JOHN: No, the jolly Smuckers. I'm trying to keep my sense of
28   humor.

29   ABNER: Right. OK, Mr. Smuckers, I want to know if I am
30   covered for medical bills or a visit to the hospital.

31   JOHN: I'll check for you, sir. *(Goes through notebook.)*

32   ABNER: It's painful and I'm incapacitated.

33   JOHN: *(Irritated)* **I said I'll check.**

34   ABNER: Check, check.

35   JOHN: Ah, here it is. You have up to fifty thousand dollars in

1   property damage and free road service and towing up to
2   twenty-five dollars.
3   ABNER: No, no, no. Not car insurance. My hospitalization
4   plan. Am I covered for this?
5   JOHN: Policy number please.
6   ABNER: I gave you my policy number! It's *(Reads)* 847362-A-
7   8990054-B.
8   JOHN: *(He writes it as ABNER speaks, then calls out triumphantly.)*
9   Hey, I found it. Right here with my morning toast.
10   ABNER: Hope it's whole wheat. You probably need the fiber.
11   JOHN: No need to be surly.
12   ABNER: I'm not being surly. I just want to know . . . look,
13   forget it. I'll take care of it. I'll pick up the tab myself.
14   JOHN: Tab's a low-cal drink.
15   ABNER: I know, I know . . .
16   JOHN: And if you do need car insurance we also operate the
17   Highways and Byways Car Insurance Company.
18   ABNER: I don't have a car.
19   JOHN: *(Still selling)* My uncle has a used car dealership —
20   Claude the Cuckoo Canadian.
21   ABNER: *(Shakes head.)* Good-by, Mr. Smuckers. *(He hangs up*
22   *the phone. ABNER slams phone down. Unfortunately, he has*
23   *one hand on the phone and he hurts himself again. He shouts*
24   *in pain and shakes hand in air and clenches and unclenches*
25   *fist. JOHN is going through some papers. ABNER has calmed*
26   *down. Bites lip, looks at phone, then picks it up and starts dialing.*
27   *We hear the phone ring. JOHN picks it up.)* Acme High Life
28   Insurance and Happy Times Hospitalization? John
29   Smuckers , please . . .
30   JOHN: John Smuckers speaking. *(Brief pause, then smile.)*
31   Abner? *(Curtain or blackout)*
32
33
34
35

#28

It's Not the Coughin' — It's the Coffin They Carry You Off In

CAST: ANNOUNCER, male or female, On-Stage or Off; JOE, anywhere from twenty-five to sixty, a constant, heavy smoker who, unsurprisingly, coughs a lot; his LUNGS, dressed completely in gray.

SETTING: Seating arrangements for both performers. A table with a telephone. A pad will be needed for a performer to use, if desired.

ANNOUNCER: No doubt about it, one of the greatest causes of early death in our nation is smoking. The country is becoming very aware of this and is taking steps to do something about it. Airlines, restaurants, auditoriums and other enclosed places where people gather have instituted no smoking areas for the benefit of nonsmokers. It has become a very controversial issue all over the land. And it brings all sorts of conflicts no matter who or what is involved.

(OPENING: JOE enters coughing and sits down. He is closely followed by his LUNGS, who sits nearby. He listens and looks with disgust at JOE, who is still coughing. He finally stops.)

LUNGS: Hey, I think you're off a tiny bit. You're coughing in the key of B flat, which is the condition I'll be in if you keep on smoking. I'll be flat.

JOE: *(With irritation)* I got a funny pair of lungs. Maybe I can get you a job in Vegas somewhere.

LUNGS: I'm only thinking of you ... and maybe myself a little bit. You're doing four packs a day now.

JOE: Who's counting?

1   LUNGS: I am. Look at me. Gray as the Los Angeles skyline.
2   ,   And I've never even been in a coal mine. I'm gray all over.
3   JOE: On you it looks good. *(JOE goes into a coughing spasm.*
4   *With each cough, LUNGS cringes and glares at him.)*
5   LUNGS: Beautiful. *(Shakes head.)* TB or not TB? — that is the
6   question.
7   JOE: Look, I've got a lot of tension. Besides, I can quit any
8   time I like. It's just something to keep my lips occupied.
9   *(Chuckles.)*
10 LUNGS: Learn to play a bugle.
11 JOE: I'll learn to play reveille, wake myself up. *(Yawns)*
12 LUNGS: You know why you're always tired don't you?
13 JOE: No, but you'll tell me.
14 LUNGS: Let me explain. Smoking impairs the body's utilization
15   of oxygen and reduces the level of vitamin C. Ergo —
16   energy loss.
17 JOE: *(Disgustedly)* Yeah, yeah.
18 LUNGS: All that rasping, gasping, coughing, spitting,
19   gargling.
20 JOE: Sounds like the law firm I used to work for.
21 LUNGS: Look, try a substitute. Hold a pen in your hand, eat
22   popcorn, munch on carrot sticks, chew gum — sugar-free,
23   of course.
24 JOE: How would it look if I lit up a carrot stick? *(Chuckles)*
25 LUNGS: A typical avoidance attitude. Read somewhere that
26   you and others smoke automatically. Some guy said you
27   should put an elastic band around your pack of cigarettes
28   so you'd think before you pried one free.
29 JOE: A friend of mine tried that once. Ended up smoking
30   three packs of elastics a day. *(Laughs and ends up coughing.)*
31 LUNGS: OK, OK. Look, if you don't care about yourself and
32   me, what about your family and friends? There is such
33   a thing as passive cancer, you know.
34 JOE: Yeah, I hear talk.
35 LUNGS: They can get cancer just by being near you in a

1   closed room.

2   JOE: Have them tell the usher to change their seats.

3   LUNGS: Look, you may have already infected someone,
4   sending them toward their doom. That's manslaughter,
5   a punishable offense. *(Calls off in the manner of McGarrett*
6   *of "Hawaii Five-O.")* **Book 'em, Danno.**

7   JOE: Police, eh? Mess with me and I'll cop a plea. *(Laughs*
8   *and ends up coughing once again. LUNGS shakes his head in*
9   *dismay. The phone rings; JOE picks it up.)*

10 JOE: *(Into phone)* **Yeah?** *(Listens)* **Right. I smoke your company's**
11   **brand. Unlucky Strikes. Right. That's right, four packs a**
12   **day.** *(Listens)* **Appear in a full-page national advertising**
13   **campaign in twenty magazines? Sure. I'd love it.** *(Listens)*
14   **That's good money. Sure. When?** *(Listens)* **Ten in the**
15   **morning? Impossible. I don't stop smoking until eleven.**
16   *(Chuckles and coughs.)* **I'll get back to you.** *(Hangs up phone.*
17   *JOE yawns and lies back in chair or on sofa.)*

18 LUNGS: Well, that extended conversation really wore you
19   out. You're in great shape. If you didn't cough you'd get
20   no exercise at all.

21 JOE: *(Irritated)* **You're starting to bug me. Why don't you get**
22   **out of here?**

23 LUNGS: All right, all right.

24 JOE: Yeah, get lost. Go, go, go! *(JOE takes out pack of cigarettes*
25   *from pocket. LUNGS stands up reluctantly.)*

26 LUNGS: OK, I'll go. But remember, *(His voice drops threateningly)*
27   **if I go . . .** *(warningly)* **I'm taking you with me.**

28 JOE: Yeah, yeah. *(JOE watches as LUNGS exits, and launches*
29   *into a violent coughing spasm.)*

30
31
32
33
34
35

#29

The Mobile Therapist

CAST: ANNOUNCER, male or female, On-Stage or Off; Mr. KROM, the driving therapist, calm, sure of himself, but given to occasional frantic outbursts due to the actions of his patient behind the wheel. Aged thirty to fifty; ARNIE, the motorist afflicted with various road phobias. Aged thirty to fifty.

SETTING: Two seats, representing a car's front seat, facing the audience. A steering wheel in its proper place would add to the imagery.

ANNOUNCER: There are many motorists with driving phobias. But that's why there are therapists like Dr. Herkie Krom. Let's meet him.
(OPENING: KROM is seated in the passenger seat, looking at a slip of paper. ARNIE enters the scene. He is hesitant about approaching the car.)

KROM: *(Affably)* **Arnie, come on. Get in.** *(He pats the driver's seat.)*

ARNIE: Right. Morning, Dr. Krom. *(He slides onto his seat.)*

KROM: *(Reading from paper)* **Arnie Whistner. Fear of crossing over bridges, going through tunnels, driving on high-speed highways.**

ARNIE: *(Nods, smiles sheepishly.)* **That's about it.**

KROM: Have no fear, old Doctor Krom is here. Now I want you to sit back ... *(ARNIE does so)* **take a deep breath** *(ARNIE does)* **and close your eyes.** *(ARNIE obeys.)* **I only suggest the last one when we're parked, not whizzing at fifty-five.** *(He smiles. It is his standard joke.)* **OK, Arnie, start 'er up.** *(ARNIE comes alive, turns the key. In the absence of a motor sound effect, we know the car is going when KROM slams*

1 *back against the seat.)* **Easy, Arnie, you've got a full hour**
2 **session.** *(ARNIE calms down and relaxes.)*
3 **ARNIE: How'm I doing?**
4 **KROM: I'll tell you more when we get out of the driveway.**
5 **OK, turn here. Remember, you're perfectly safe. We have**
6 **an invisible steel curtain around the car so nothing can**
7 **harm you.**
8 **ARNIE:** *(Smiles)* **Great!**
9 **KROM:** *(After glancing at note)* **You have quite a driving record.**
10 **Never think you have hang-ups.**
11 **ARNIE: Some sneaky patrolmen nabbed me once or twice.**
12 **KROM: Speeding while driving a football team's bus. How**
13 **fast were you going?**
14 **ARNIE: Don't know. The speedometer only registered when**
15 **all four wheels touched the ground.**
16 **KROM: That's really moving. Any accidents?**
17 **ARNIE: No. When I approached the city line I put down the**
18 **comic book I was reading.**
19 **KROM:** *(Taking it in stride)* **Safety first.**
20 **ARNIE: And when I got into the city I made my girl friend**
21 **get off my lap.**
22 **KROM: Your copilot. I understand.** *(Sneaks a quick peek at*
23 *ARNIE. Then his body snaps back. He turns to the driver.)*
24 **Arnie, you passed a stop sign and you're breaking the**
25 **speed limit. I want to cure you of your driving fears, not**
26 ***bring* fear into the hearts of other drivers.**
27 **ARNIE:** *(Comfortable now)* **Maybe I can scare up a few more**
28 **customers for you, Doc.** *(Chuckles.)*
29 **KROM: OK, take this on-ramp. Careful. There's lots of traffic.**
30 *(He snaps back into his seat.)* **Remember, you can't get hurt.**
31 **There's the invisible steel curtain around you.**
32 **ARNIE: Gotcha.**
33 **KROM: How you feeling?** *(Body rocks back and forth.)*
34 **ARNIE: Great. Hey, I got that steel curtain, right?**
35 **KROM: Right. You weaved in and out. You're breaking the**

1		speed limit. *(Pause as ARNIE drives on.)* **You know there's**
2		**a theory about reckless drivers. Going too fast. It**
3		**maintains that drivers are bad drivers because they are**
4		**ugly people. They have just been told they are unwanted**
5		**at the place they just stopped and are driving fast to get**
6		**to some other place ... where they will also be rejected.**
7		**I may have to classify you as one of those people.**
8	ARNIE:	**People like me ... sometimes.**
9	KROM:	*(Heatedly)* **It says you have a rotten personality and**
10		**don't bathe frequently enough and that's why no one**
11		**wants you around.**
12	ARNIE:	*(A little hurt)* **Don't you want me around?**
13	KROM:	**For seventy-five bucks an hour I'd like Godzilla**
14		**around.**
15	ARNIE:	**Oh ... oh ... here's a bridge. I'm taking it in a breeze.**
16		**Watch this.** *(He smiles confidently. He pushes hard on the gas*
17		*pedal sending KROM back in his seat. They continue on like*
18		*this. KROM looks out and panic starts to show in his face. He*
19		*clings to the seat and gulps, terrified.)* **A piece of cake. Who**
20		**cares about that water down there a couple of hundred**
21		**feet?** *(KROM shakes head and holds hand over his eyes.)* **And**
22		**here's that long, long tunnel. I want that tunnel!** *(He begins*
23		*singing.)* **"Many brave hearts are asleep in the deep, so**
24		**beware ... be ... eee ... eee ... ware."** *(As he hits the low*
25		*bass note, KROM slumps deep in his seat.)* **Nothing to it.** *(Takes*
26		*hands off wheel.)* **Look, Ma, no hands!** *(This is too much for*
27		*KROM.)*
28	KROM:	**Pull over.**
29	ARNIE:	**I still got time left.**
30	KROM:	**Forget it. It's on the house. No charge!**
31	ARNIE:	**You cured me for free. Beautiful!**
32	KROM:	**Let's change seats. I'll drive back.** *(They change seats*
33		*with a trembling KROM now behind the wheel.)*
34	ARNIE:	**I'm cured! I love driving!** *(KROM looks skyward and*
35		*glances at ARNIE. Then upwards again.)*

1   KROM: Please forgive me, State Highway Patrol. I'll make
2   it up to you. I promise. *(Starts car and he drives off, shaken,*
3   *very hesitantly, with an enthusiastic ARNIE grinning as big a*
4   *grin as he can.)*
5
6
7
8
9
10
11
12
13
14
15
16
17
18
19
20
21
22
23
24
25
26
27
28
29
30
31
32
33
34
35

#30

Those Good Old Radio-Active Days

6   *CAST:*   ANNOUNCER, male or female; On-Stage or Off; TED and
7   BILL, two old friends brought together after not seeing each
8   other for a number of years. Both have hit the sixty-year-old
9   mark. Their conversation is friendly, filled with reminiscenses
10   as they travel down memory lane via the old-time radio route.

12   *SETTING:*   Sofa or two easy chairs where men sit, close enough to
13   each other to be able to talk easily.

15   **ANNOUNCER:**   **The Golden Age of Radio is dead, they say.**
16   **And they're probably right. But it lives in the memory of**
17   **many of our citizens. It occurred during the thirties and**
18   **forties and still brings fond moments of recall to people**
19   **who sometimes try to recapture the fun and joy of the**
20   **times as the family gathered in the living room around**
21   **the big upright.**
22   *(OPENING: TED and BILL walk in together slowly, plop into*
23   *their chairs [sofa] and heave deep sighs.)*
24   **BILL:**   **Hey, it's great seeing you again, Ted.**
25   **TED:**   **Same here.**
26   **BILL:**   **Nice of Gerry to invite the old gang here for a little**
27   **reunion.**
28   **TED:**   **The old Royals.**
29   **BILL:**   **We were pretty good.**
30   **TED:**   **Sometimes *very* good.**
31   **BILL:**   **Right. You and the wife get out much?**
32   **TED:**   **Nope. No place to go. Can't stand the music out there**
33   **... or the movies.**
34   **BILL:**   **Or television.**
35   **TED:**   **Yeah. I still miss the old radio days.**

1 BILL: Me too. You know some nights when I'm home alone,
2   I look at the television set for about ten minutes ... and
3   it's not even turned on.
4 TED: The times are catching up to you. And me too.
5 BILL: But instead of seeing things, I'm hearing things. Like
6   ...(Becomes announcer) "Jack Armstrong, the All-
7   American Boy."
8 TED: Great show. (Sings) "Wave the flag for Hudson High,
9   boys."
10 TED and BILL: (Unison) "Show them how we stand ..."
11 BILL: And they got around. Jack in Africa ... South Pacific ...
12   stars on the football field.
13 TED: Jack ... Betty and Billy Fairfield and Uncle Jim.
14 BILL: I always liked Betty Fairfield. Great voice. I always
15   figured she looked like Theresa Duncan, who lived down
16   the street.
17 TED: Either Theresa or Hedy Lamarr.
18 BILL: Same thing in my book.
19 TED: Know what was nice? You didn't have twenty sponsors
20   shouting at you in those fifteen minutes.
21 BILL: Right. Only one sponsor. Remember who it was?
22 TED: Wheaties ... from General Mills.
23 BILL: You know for the longest time I thought General Mills
24   was a retired Army officer, maybe a West Point football
25   hero who made Wheaties for the sole purpose of creating
26   bigger, better boys.
27 TED: Tell you another show I liked. Lamont Cranston.
28   (Announcer's voice) "Who knows what evil lurks in the hearts
29   of men?"
30 BILL: "The Shadow knows." What the heck, I would know too
31   if I could be invisible every time I wanted to.
32 TED: I always wanted to be invisible to find out about the evil
33   in the heart of Beverly Sampson.
34 BILL: Sally Hamilton.
35 TED: Or even Theresa Duncan who lived down the street.

1	BILL:	Some kind of girl, Theresa was.
2	TED:	They have so many crime shows on TV these days, and I
3		think it all started with Dick Tracy.
4	BILL:	That was the time when they had real criminals with
5		great names. Pretty Boy Floyd ... Baby Face Nelson ...
6	TED:	My favorite bad guy was on the Tracy show. Chopper
7		Grimes.
8	BILL:	He was mean.
9	TED:	I remember him calling out to Tracy during a gun fight.
10		"You'll never take me alive, Tracy."
11	BILL:	And he was right. Got hit about seventy times, but he
12		was tough, snarling and battling to the bitter end.
13	TED:	I remember we wore our G-man badges at half-mast
14		for three days.
15	BILL:	There were good crime shows on then. Gangbusters.
16	TED:	Mr. District Attorney.
17	BILL:	One guy I didn't like was Mr. Keen, Tracer of Lost
18		Persons.
19	TED:	Right. A busybody, you know? Always nosing around.
20	BILL:	You know, if a guy wanted to get lost, let him. Probably
21		had a good reason.
22	TED:	Unless he traced Theresa Duncan ...
23	BILL:	*(Laughing)* ... who lived down the street.
24	TED:	Speaking of lovely ladies, how about Little Orphan
25		Annie?
26	BILL:	Popular kid. Was in the comic strips at the same time.
27	TED:	Funny eyes. Never changed her dress.
28	BILL:	Catch me dancing close with her.
29	TED:	And she had that dog ... what was it? ... Sandy ... the
30		dog with the bad news bark.
31	BILL:	But she offered a lot of gifts ... you know ... code
32		rings.
33	TED:	*(Does Jackie Gleason)* And the Little Orphan Annie
34		Shakeup Mug, boys and girls.
35	BILL:	You know who could scare you? The guy on Inner

1   Sanctum.

2   TED: *(In sepulchral voice)* **"This is Raymond, your host."**

3   BILL: **Love that squeaking door.**

4   TED: **I still remember one of his sign-offs.** *(Ominous voice)*

5   **"Remember — voodoo unto others as you would have**

6   **others voodoo unto you."**

7   BILL: *(Laughing)* **A classic that will live forever.**

8   TED: **Great comedy shows too. Bob Hope Show.**

9   BILL: **Bing Crosby Radio Music Hall.**

10   TED: **Lots of adventure shows. Tom Mix.**

11   BILL: **Big Town.**

12   TED: **The Green Hornet.**

13   BILL: **I Love a Mystery.**

14   TED: **The Lone Ranger.**

15   BILL: **I wonder who that masked man was?**

16   TED: **There was one comedy show I liked that never made it**

17   **big. But I liked it. Meet Mr. Meek.**

18   BILL: **Good show. So was Henry Aldrich.** *(Calling)* **Hen-n-n-ry**

19   **Aldrich!**

20   TED: *(Calling in cracked voice of character)* **Coming, Mother!**

21   BILL: **Yeah . . . good stuff.**

22   TED: **Takes you back.** *(There is a pause here as they let the happy*

23   *memories sift through their minds.)*

24   BILL: **Happy times.**

25   TED: **Lots of memories. Good ones.**

26   BILL: **The innocent years they call them now.**

27   TED: **None of the filth you see today that they're throwing**

28   **out at the kids.**

29   BILL: **It's a shame that they missed the decent, funny and . . .**

30   **yes . . . romantic times we had.**

31   TED: **True, true.** *(Another pause to do some hasty recalling of good*

32   *times past.)*

33   BILL: *(Looks at watch.)* **Hey, it's getting late.**

34   TED: **Right. Shall we join the ladies?**

35   BILL: **Sure . . . or even Theresa Duncan who lives down the**

1   street.
2   **TED: You said it.** *(They get up and walk off happily, bathed in the*
3   *memories of times they enjoyed. Then they begin singing as they*
4   *leave.)*
5   **BILL and TED: "Wave the flag for Hudson High, boys. Show**
6   **them how we stand . . ."**
7
8
9
10
11
12
13
14
15
16
17
18
19
20
21
22
23
24
25
26
27
28
29
30
31
32
33
34
35

TWO WOMEN

#31

Swinging Singles Hideaway

CAST: ANNOUNCER, male or female, On-Stage or Off; SALLY and SUE. They are both attractive and friendly and are good friends recalling last summer's vacation.

SETTING: Two chairs where performers can sit in casual fashion. SUE reads from her diary; SALLY acknowledges lines and makes comments.

ANNOUNCER: The biggest increases in the travel agency business are getaway resorts for swinging singles. Every year, more and more of the single set, the once-married, and the want-to-be-married go away for fun, adventure and, hopefully, a future spouse. What kind of people try their luck in singles resorts? Girls like these two single girls — Sally and Sue.

SALLY: I'm glad you kept a diary of our getaway last year.

SUE: Hey, it was lots of fun.

SALLY: Go ahead and read it. I like to relive happy times.

SUE: Fine. *(Reads)* Friday — 7 o'clock — Check-in time at front desk of Happiness Hotel.

SALLY: Remember all those bellboys getting into a big battle to carry our suitcases?

SUE: Sure do. Two of them were carried out on stretchers.

SALLY: Right. Go on.

SUE: *(Reads)* 8 p.m. — Free soda and chips at Get-Acquainted Time in the hotel's famous Free Soda and Chips at Get-Acquainted Time Room. 8:30 p.m. — World renowned Happiness Hotel hostesses perform their famed bikini cancan in lobby. 9 p.m. — First aid for the overly excitable.

1   SALLY: Those guys were dropping like flies.

2   SUE: *(Reads)* 10 p.m. — Entertainment provided by the

3   Greenwich Village Mixed Yodeling Choraleers.

4   SALLY: I never heard such high notes in my life.

5   SUE: And the girls were pretty good too.

6   SALLY: True, true.

7   SUE: *(Reads)* 11 p.m. — Dance to the exciting music of Martin

8   Mackinaw's Merry Matadors' eighty-six piece orchestra.

9   SALLY: Nice band, but I got sick of all those sambas, and

10   tangos and congas.

11   SUE: True. But it was nice when they lifted the short marimba

12   player up on their shoulders to see the dancers and they

13   sang "Jose, Can You See?"

14   SALLY: That was inspiring.

15   SUE: *(Reads)* Midnight — Pre-bedtime snack consisting of

16   peppermint demitasse, chow mein surprise and boiled

17   leopard lip sandwiches steeped in jellybean sauce. 12:30 —

18   Stomach pumps all around.

19   SALLY: I still have mine.

20   SUE: *(Reads)* Saturday, 8 a.m. — After breakfast a guided tour

21   to the top of Mount Festive for a breathtaking view of

22   Tom Selleck.

23   SALLY: Yeah, but he never showed up.

24   SUE: But the tour guide was cute.

25   SALLY: Yeah, he won the Jamie Farr Look-a-Like Contest.

26   SUE: Won by a nose. *(Reads)* 10 a.m. until noon — Downhill

27   Single Senior Citizens Bobsled Race.

28   SALLY: Remember what the band played on the PA system?

29   SUE: No, what?

30   SALLY: "I Want to Be Around to Pick Up the Pieces."

31   SUE: Right. *(Reads)* 1 p.m. — Luncheon consisting of

32   succotash sweetmeats cut in the shape of Madonna. 2 p.m.

33   — To the pool to watch Edgar Lunger stay under water

34   for twenty minutes. 2:20 — Poolside services for Edgar

35   Lunger.

1   SALLY: *(Sadly)* That sort of put a damper on everything.

2   SUE: But only for awhile because *(Reads)* at 4:30 there was a

3   belly dancing exhibition by the world-famous Feejilah.

4   SALLY: I talked to him later. Nice guy.

5   SUE: *(Reads)* 7 p.m. — Dinner followed by Broadway-style

6   show featuring fortunetelling by Zabora who peered

7   deeply into a bald man's head, a lacrosse game played

8   on trained donkeys and the first appearance of the

9   County Riflemen's Club.

10 SALLY: Yeah, I think they were the ones who sneaked

11   upstairs and rifled our rooms.

12 SUE: They *did* look a little shifty. *(Reads)* 10:30 — Game time

13   — played Pin the Tail on the Bellboy, Spin the Hockey

14   Stick and Bobbing for Short Guys.

15 SALLY: I got stuck with Little Larry.

16 SUE: He *was* a trifle undersized.

17 SALLY: He was so short he had to climb a ladder to tip his hat.

18 SUE: *(Reads)* Midnight — Make a New Friend Hour.

19 SALLY: I was still stuck with Little Larry. He was so short he

20   never really ever saw a parade.

21 SUE: OK, OK, enough with the short jokes.

22 SALLY: Right. But he never came up to my expectations.

23 SUE: Right. Moving right along . . . *(Reads)* Sunday — 8 a.m.

24   Breakfast consisting of anything left over from Friday

25   and Saturday. 11 a.m. — Turkish bath. Four trained brush

26   salesmen climb into a vat to bathe a Turk. Noon — Lunch

27   consisting of broccoli tidbits and a Jell-O mold in the

28   shape of Meryl Streep.

29 SALLY: Not bad, especially with the peanut butter dip.

30 SUE: *(Reads)* 2 p.m. — Meeting of the Thirty-Eight-and-Over

31   Club. 3 p.m. — Meeting of girls who aren't so buxom. 5 p.m.

32   — Silly Putty sculpting exhibition performed to one of

33   Eddie Murphy's comedy routines.

34 SALLY: Laugh? I thought I'd never start.

35 SUE: *(Reads)* 10 p.m. — Snare a Sweetie Sweepstakes. For

1	men only. Wearing a bathing suit, a girl named Shirley
2	is covered with mayonnaise, men are given leather
3	gloves, the gun sounds and Shirley runs for her life
4	through the lobby.
5	SALLY: She ended up with a pretty nice guy. Talk about
6	dumb luck.
7	SUE: But she paid the price. Those ugly leather stains all
8	over her body. *(Reads)* 11 p.m. — Lucky drawing — prize —
9	free transportation home. Winner is stuffed into the
10	mouth of a cannon and shot home. *(Looks hard at SALLY.)*
11	SALLY: *(Defensively)* OK, so I cheated. But it beats the bus and
12	it's a heck of a lot cheaper.
13	SUE: Going back next year?
14	SALLY: Maybe. You?
15	SUE: Those broccoli tidbits *were* good.
16	SALLY: Especially with the peanut butter dip.
17	SUE: Let's go.
18	SALLY: You got it. *(They shake hands on it.)*
19	SUE: *If* . . . we're still single.
20	SALLY: *(Laughing in friendly fashion)* Then you'll just have to
21	go alone.
22	SUE: *(Getting it)* Me? *Me?* I didn't tell you about this guy at
23	work. Crazy about me. Tall, blond, good-looking. I know
24	he's going to ask me out. And I'm going to say yes. And
25	then who knows?
26	SALLY: *(Realizes SUE's sort of bluffing.)* We'll go together. *(They*
27	*shake hands.)*
28	SUE: Together.
29	SALLY: The two swinging singles.
30	SUE: Good broccoli tidbits.
31	SALLY: Right. Especially with the peanut butter dip. *(They*
32	*walk off happily together.)*
33	
34	
35	

#32

Unusual Unknown Tours for Tourists

CAST: ANNOUNCER, male or female, On-Stage or Off; TERRI and TINA, both young and quite enthusiastic about the tours they are touting.

SETTING: Plain stage or table with papers containing lines they can read. They can stand or sit as they perform.

ANNOUNCER: There are lots of rather offbeat tours that go on in this country — trips for tourists that are relatively unknown. For instance, did you know that Chicago has a tour of all the famous and infamous gangland activities that took place there in the twenties? For a fee you can see Al Capone's house, the Clark Street garage where the St. Valentine's Day Massacre took place and the theater where John Dillinger saw a movie just before being gunned down by the FBI.

There are tours available right in New York City you may not be aware of. To fill us in, here are Terri and Tina, the two operators of Off-the-Wall Tours for Tourists.

TERRI: Thank you. What do we have first, Tina?

TINA: The Subway Olympics. Rush hours from 8 to 9:30 a.m. and 4 to 5:30 p.m. are the times to witness this Stone Age struggle in a modern, mechanized world.

TERRI: Watch as three hundred overweight people in winter clothing jam into a car built for two hundred slim folks in tee shirts.

TINA: See the shoving, pushing and clawing as contestants fight for the great prize — a seat!

TERRI: You may even witness a minor catastrophe as the mechanism breaks down.

1   TINA: The lights go off.
2   TERRI: The temperature rises twenty degrees.
3   TINA: You can see this angry, snarling mob trapped under-
4   ground.
5   TERRI: In case of trouble, the emergency exit is in Philadelphia.
6   TINA: The Secret Beauty Contest — suggested for men only.
7   TERRI: Stroll along Madison or Fifth Avenue at noontime
8   and be an unofficial judge, peering at the passing parade
9   of sweet secretaries, torrid typists and voluptuous vice
10   presidents from ad agencies and insurance companies.
11   TINA: It's a chance to stack up your opinions against the
12   experts, who, disguised as interior decorators, stroll
13   among these lovelies and gauge the amount of fleshy
14   acreage on display or packed tightly into clinging
15   garments.
16   TERRI: The kind men like!
17   TINA: Finals are held in late August when competition is
18   really keen.
19   TERRI: Winners in each judging category receive a pair of
20   matching hurricane lamps and a bottle of suntan lotion.
21   TINA: LaGuardia Airport Field Trip!
22   TERRI: Take a limousine ride out to the runway at LaGuardia
23   and howl with glee as giant airplanes skim three feet over
24   your roof as they try for a landing this side of Flushing Bay
25   and the East River.
26   TINA: Bring the folks.
27   TERRI: A fashion show for stewardesses and an Eddie
28   Rickenbacker Look-a-Like contest are Tuesday attractions.
29   TINA: Thursday is crash landing day.
30   TERRI: Manhattan Boat Trip!
31   TINA: A three-hour boat trip completely around Manhattan
32   Island is a must.
33   TERRI: Now these are not the big Circle Line trips.
34   TINA: These are dinghies supplied by the Flotsam and Jetsam
35   Balsam and Chandelier works of Hoboken.

1   TERRI: Dip your hand into the Hudson River as you skim
2   lazily over the water.
3   TINA: If rash appears, call doctor immediately.
4   TERRI: Watch as fish rise to the surface — coughing.
5   TINA: Great fun for the inoculated!
6   TERRI: Also, a pleasurable voyage for tourists with only *two*
7   hours to kill — a boat trip completely around John Candy
8   and Roseanne Barr.
9   TINA: So, we'll be seeing you at . . .
10   TERRI: Off-the-Wall Tours for Tourists.
11   TINA and TERRI: *(Cheerily)* Have a nice trip!
12
13
14
15
16
17
18
19
20
21
22
23
24
25
26
27
28
29
30
31
32
33
34
35

#33

Video Vaudeo Varieties

CAST: ANNOUNCER, male or female, On-Stage or Off, VICKI and VANNA.

SETTING: Long table, two chairs where VICKI and VANNA sit and read their lines. It is basically a broadcast set-up.

ANNOUNCER: The biggest boom in entertainment these days is, without a doubt, home videos. Television networks and independent companies are living with great apprehension as sales of these home videos skyrocket, cutting into their market share.

There seems to be no limit on the areas that are covered in home videos, whereas networks have federal authorities and their own offices of standards and practices — arbiters of good taste — overseeing the material presented. Though home videos offer the standard films and TV shows, there are some that might be considered shall we say ... weird or offbeat. With that in mind, here are Vicki and Vanna with the latest in off-the-wall videos for home viewers.

(OPENING: Girls are seated at table reading from scripts, facing the audience.)

VICKI: Thank you, Virgil. *(Virginia)* Well, Vanna, what do we have to lead off this latest selection of home video releases?

VANNA: A gem, Vicki. It's called "Corn on the Macabre" — a grim, well-documented tale of an ambitious middle-class youth's struggle to reach the top in the highly competitive undertaking game.

VICKI: I understand there is stiff competition in that field.

1 VANNA: Right you are, Vicki. From his beginning as a part-
2   time reckless driver for a funeral home in Winding Sheet,
3   Nebraska, the hero, Farley Shroud, epitomizes what is
4   right and what is wrong with our capitalistic free enterprise
5   system.
6 VICKI: He eventually achieves success operating a chain of
7   coin-operated funeral homes. "Like an automat or an
8   arcade," he explains, "but the windows are larger."
9 VANNA: As an ironic dénouement, he is run over by a
10   berserk hearse driver and is buried in an unmarked
11   orange crate in Potter's Field. Lana Sepulchral directed.
12 VICKI: "The Niceman Cometh" — a surprisingly delightful
13   little look at a perenially happy wishing well attendant
14   who spreads smiles and optimism while passing out free
15   lollipops at divorce hearings. Produced by Smiley
16   Fenton, accused by many critics of being "soft-headed
17   and silly" for his cheerful attitudes, the film nevertheless
18   contains such bitingly realistic moments as the one in
19   which the hero, Laugh-a-lot Shugue, kicks a Good Humor
20   man on Sesame Street and risks losing his popularity by
21   agreeing to write hold-up notes for illiterate bank
22   robbers.
23 VANNA: Here's one for all you fans of the theater of the
24   absurd. It's called "Waiting for Go-Go." This low-budget
25   opus deals with the revelations and ruminations of a pair
26   of drifters who sit waist deep in a laundry hamper, hiding
27   from reality as they try to find themselves and life's true
28   meaning.
29 VICKI: The rambling, discursive dialog, oftentimes deep,
30   sometimes irritatingly banal, covers such topics as
31   riverboats, autopsies on furry creatures, breakfast
32   cereals, curling and the true meaning of lassitude.
33 VANNA: Playing the roles of Slick and Slack, two
34   ex-vaudevillians confused by life's realities, are Slick and
35   Slack, two ex-vaudevillians confused by life's realities.

1	**VICKI:** "Anatomy of a Belch" — capitalizing on the world's
2	preoccupation with food, this musical documentary
3	follows a kosher pickle from tongue to esophagus to
4	intestinal tract to a rousing climax with an eruptive
5	eructation resembling a Vesuvian blow-off.
6	**VANNA:** Not for the queasy.
7	**VICKI:** However, technical brilliance and skillful musical
8	interpolation of appropriate tunes will command
9	admiration. Watch for the barbershop quartet's soulful
10	version of "Alimentary, My Dear Watson."
11	**VANNA:** Released by the Latvian Organic Health Foods High
12	Life Film and Sunflower Seeds and Bicarbonate
13	Company.
14	**VICKI:** Finally, we have "Hoodstock Music Festival."
15	**VANNA:** This on-the-scene film record of the now-famous
16	festival for freaked-out over-fifties, is vivid, graphic and
17	colorful. The unblinking eye of the camera watches these
18	establishment types waltz to the music of Harry Horlick's
19	A&P Gypsies, overdose on brewer's yeast and Geritol and
20	strut about wearing banners proclaiming the glories of
21	Wayne King, the Waltz King.
22	**VICKI:** Highlight occurs when a roving band of drop-out,
23	gray-haired business executives invades a nearby farm,
24	fills a bag with one hundred pounds of crab grass and
25	sends it to Jane Fonda to make a movie with a message.
26	**VANNA:** And that's it for today, friends.
27	**VICKI:** This is Vicki... *(Holds up two fingers in V for victory*
28	*sign)*
29	**VANNA:** And this is Vanna... *(Does the same)*
30	**VICKI:** Saying happy video viewing one and all. *(End with big,*
31	*happy, toothy smiles.)*
32	
33	
34	
35	

#34

The Gracious Guide to Good Gulping

CAST: ANNOUNCER, male or female, Off-Stage; AMY and BABS. No specific physical type or age group.

SETTING: Desk or table with two chairs. Mike set-up might be used.

ANNOUNCER: Many visitors to our fair city complain of being unable to find a good restaurant at reasonable prices. To help them, our own Amy and Babs, who know the restaurant business from A to B, present "The Gracious Guide to Good Gulping." Girls, if you'll start with the appetizer...

AMY: We certainly will. Babs, you want to begin?

BABS: I'd like to tell our listeners *(Viewers)* about Johnny the Referee's place, situated just across the street from the old Fisticuffs Arena. If you like action with your food, this is the place. All the waiters are punchy ex-fighters and you should see the wild fun begin when Johnny rings the dinner gong.

AMY: I bet it's a riot.

BABS: Something to see. Specialty of the house is pound cake, pounded to your order by seven ex-middleweight contenders. Another recommended item is Canvasback Duck. Back to you, Amy.

AMY: If you folks like to see celebrities munching their meals, I suggest you visit Benny's Place. El Brendel, Henry Armetta, Sonny Tufts, Professor Backwards, Johnny Downs and Sliding Billy Watson have all eaten here — once. Geographical specialties include Rock-Ribbed Coast of Chow Mein and Roast Long Island Tear

1   Duct. And for a rare taste treat, try their Double Breast
2   of Raincoat.
3   BABS: They don't have entertainment there anymore, do
4   they?
5   AMY: No, but every twenty minutes a buxom waitress in a
6   tight uniform walks slowly through the room.
7   BABS: A place I've always liked is the Silver Tassel, situated
8   at the corner of Grind Lane and Gypsy Rose Lee
9   Boulevard. The house features fine American dishes
10   whose phone numbers are printed legibly on the backs
11   of their diaphanous tunics. See your steaks heated up
12   through the open glass kitchen by the famous Radio City
13   Cookettes. A twenty-seven course buffet is served every
14   month of the year except February — which has twenty-
15   eight.
16   AMY: If you like simple food, pay a visit to Ma Lisenbee's
17   Hash House. Ma serves real old American food. When Ma
18   gets rid of the old American food, she'll start serving *new*
19   American food. Ma, an ex-English teacher, serves a
20   dessert specialty — Synonym Buns, with a vintage split
21   of infinitive wine for you to swiftly drink.
22   BABS: Well, I don't have to go there. *(Chuckles)* I already
23   speak very well English. But I think everyone would like
24   Birdville, just seventeen blocks from the Poltergeist Inn,
25   which has been torn down. Birdville features Oriole
26   Sandwiches Under Glass, Sauteed Hummingbird Lips,
27   and Twenty-four Blackbirds Baked In a Pie. Every Friday
28   a guest celebrity loudmouth who has spouted off to the
29   press comes in to eat Crow and Humble Magpie. For your
30   listening and dancing pleasure they have an intimate
31   trio led by Joseph Intimate which entertains until you
32   get tired of "Malaguena."
33   AMY: Why not try Mrs. Simple's American Type Home-Like,
34   Down-Home, Working Person's Restaurant, just forty
35   miles from the heart of the city? Unassuming decor makes

1   you feel at ease instantly. It's a home away from home.
2   There are shoes under the table, ashes on the floor and
3   dirt under the rugs. Mrs. Simple has been given ten days
4   to clean the place up.
5   BABS: Seeking a cozy spot where you can express yourself in
6   endearing terms as you snuggle up to your loved one?
7   AMY: *(Eagerly)* I am!
8   BABS: Well, then you go right over to the Clandestine Room
9   of the Hotel Smooch. That's the place. Soft lights, soft
10   music and soft rolls add to the romantic mood. Specialty
11   of the house is their dessert — heated honey buns
12   smothered with candied syrup. Kosher cuisine in
13   candlelight dining. Your chance to enjoy a knish in the
14   dark.
15   AMY: And that about wraps it up.
16   BABS: So, gracious gulping to all. *(The girls pick up their things,*
17   *stand up and start off.)*
18   ANNOUNCER: *(Calling from Off-Stage)* That's a wrap! Where
19   you two going for lunch today? *(Girls, heading off, call back.)*
20   AMY: McDonalds. *(Any other fast food places may be used here.)*
21   BABS: We went there yesterday. Burger King — the fries are
22   better.
23   AMY: *(Arguing as they exit)* You get bigger servings at
24   McDonalds.
25   BABS: The fries ... the fries is where it's at. Burger King ...
26
27
28
29
30
31
32
33
34
35

In Sickness and in Health, Till TV Do Us Part

CAST: ANNOUNCER, male or female, On-Stage or Off; BONNIE and CONNIE.

SETTING: Table, two chairs. Girls will sit and face audience as they deliver their material.

ANNOUNCER: **A virulent sickness is raging throughout America's living rooms, courtesy of television programmers. It has reached epidemic proportions.**

In the recent past we have seen programs exploring drug addiction, crippling arthritis, alcoholism, dyslexia, compulsive smoking, depression, deafness, bulimia and anorexia.

It seems the illness trend has just about run its course and should be taken off the critical list and marked terminal. But has it? It's been reported there are still numerous other ailments not as yet tapped by the networks and independents.

And here are our TV experts, Bonnie and Connie, to tell you about some other sickness shows in the works for the upcoming season.

CONNIE: **Thank you, doctor** *(Nurse)*. *(Reading or reciting)* **Leading the ailment agenda is —**

BONNIE: **"Steal City — 1990."** *(Fill in the appropriate year.)*

CONNIE: **Compulsive crooks are caught by a hidden camera as they roam through food and department stores shoplifting toasters, coasters, forks, porks, meats, beets and a partridge in a pear tree.**

BONNIE: **Character actor Edward Heist shines as a kleptomaniac who attempts to shoplift an anvil disguised**

1	as a bread box.
2	CONNIE: He will appear later in the season in "Hernia, USA."
3	BONNIE: "Tried and Found Wanton" —
4	CONNIE: An inordinate fondness for flirtation is the topic of
5	this diverting romp sponsored by No-Doze and Oh You
6	Cologne.
7	BONNIE: A hodgepodge of offbeat peccadilloes is touched
8	upon as we visit an emotionally repressed human fly and
9	pay a call on a man who, dressed up as a box of bonbons,
10	had himself delivered to the apartment of a fashion model
11	as a candygram. And next we'll see . . .
12	CONNIE: "Hey, Fatty!"
13	BONNIE: From the gentle opening strains of the Leonard
14	Lipoid Chorus singing "The Bluebird of Flabbiness," to
15	the closing sketch where a dieter, in a fit of frustration,
16	eats his metal weight reducing belt, this hour leans
17	heavily on the nation's number one problem — obesity.
18	CONNIE: Sentimental segment features a 450-pound groom
19	who presents his 425-pound bride with a symbol of lasting
20	unity — a fried onion ring set neatly on a hamburger bun
21	and then carries her *under* the threshold as the floor
22	collapses.
23	BONNIE: "Let Hurts Put You in the Driver's Seat."
24	CONNIE: A tall chanteuse sings a low-down version of
25	"Stormy Leather," and we're off and running onto the
26	highways and byways of Whacko City.
27	BONNIE: We visit a "Christmas Club for Weirdos" where a
28	member goes to his bank each week and slaps a teller in
29	the face.
30	CONNIE: At Yuletide, a big man in a Santa suit comes down
31	the chimney and cuts him to shreds with a reindeer whip.
32	BONNIE: Self-styled masochists are seen, including the man
33	who drives in demolition derbies with his tongue wedged
34	into the slot of a filled used razor blade receptacle.
35	CONNIE: "Pardon Me — The Wild Bill Hiccough Story."

1	BONNIE:	From the first tiny spasm to the final embarrassing
2		outburst, the hiccough is explored.
3	CONNIE:	We see hiccoughers eating, testifying in court as to
4		their sanity, yodeling and kissing.
5	BONNIE:	Closing feature — the All-American Hiccough
6		Toss.
7	CONNIE:	Seven Hollywood starlets place dimes on their
8		necks, lie down and hiccough the coins through the air
9		for distance and accuracy.
10	BONNIE:	Climactic close-out brings down the house when
11		actress Raquel Couchnester places a silver dollar on her
12		neck, hiccoughs, and sends it hurtling forty feet in the
13		air through a plate glass window.
14	CONNIE:	Other ailments to be explored by upcoming specials
15		not finalized at air time include —
16	BONNIE:	Edema.
17	CONNIE:	Stuttering.
18	BONNIE:	The Heartbreak of Psoriasis.
19	CONNIE:	Galloping Acne.
20	BONNIE:	Seborrhea.
21	CONNIE:	The Ague Plague.
22	BONNIE:	Funny Fever.
23	CONNIE:	Wobbler's Gait.
24	BONNIE:	Seasickness.
25	CONNIE:	Lockjaw.
26	BONNIE:	Seasickness *with* Lockjaw.
27	CONNIE:	*(Directly)* A word to you hypochondriacs and the
28		sensitive — make sure your hospitalization plans give
29		you complete coverage.
30	BONNIE and CONNIE:	Happy viewing, TV fans!
31		
32		
33		
34		
35		

#36

Not in the Top Ten Per Cent of Their Class

CAST: ANNOUNCER, male or female, On-Stage or Off; BEBEE and PHOEBE.

SETTING: BEBEE and PHOEBE are seated at a table facing audience. If possible, girls can hold up pictures or drawings of weird individuals as they announce each name and describe the person.

ANNOUNCER: Educators recently have claimed that perhaps too much emphasis is placed on the top-ranking students in their high schools. They say that all sorts of honors and awards are heaped upon the top students, while the underachievers are ignored and are made to feel inferior, a situation that can affect them adversely in the future.

With that in mind, our two education experts, Bebee and Phoebe take this opportunity to present four leading members of the Medium-to-Low Honor Societies at area high schools.

BEBEE: *(Calls to ANNOUNCER.)* Thank you, Nigel *(Nancy)*.

PHOEBE: Greb Holtsy, twenty-three, senior at Aborigine High School, ranks 245th in a class of 244. He has four older brothers also being graduated from Aborigine somewhere way down the road. Greb is quite inactive in extra-curricular activities, having rejected memberships in three societies, preferring instead, to sit in a corner and snicker at them.

BEBEE: Greb's favorite subject is getting home from school.

PHOEBE: "It's fun," he says somberly.

BEBEE: He works after school as a night watchman in an ant

1   village.

2   PHOEBE: Next year he hopes to start going out with girls.

3   BEBEE: Mary Kra, seventeen, and quite aware of it, is known
4   for her slow wit and weird walk.

5   PHOEBE: She is a junior at the Abcedenarian School for
6   Girls, Boys and What Have You.

7   BEBEE: She is a member of the Book and Bumbling Society
8   and the Whiff, Wham and Dozing Society, specializing in
9   knitting, purling and scat singing.

10   PHOEBE: She belonged to the school's Tutu Ballet Corps,
11   but quit when she kicked off her slipper.

12   BEBEE: Mary's parents graduated last year.

13   PHOEBE: Leon J. Halomancy, seventeen, is a happy lad who
14   spends much of his days at Myxedema High yodeling the
15   blues and tossing salt over his left shoulder to ward off
16   bad luck.

17   BEBEE: His hobby is lying prone and shouting insults at
18   bluebirds.

19   PHOEBE: He is writing a monosyllabic treatise on the ethics
20   of yawning.

21   BEBEE: As his teacher says of him: "Leon someday will
22   change completely or that lad doesn't stand a chance of
23   a snowball in Hades."

24   PHOEBE: Castra Delastra, sixteen, is a top athlete, leading
25   the city last year in high jumping and low marks.

26   BEBEE: This year Castra is learning to smile and frown and
27   is doing quite well, according to her teachers.

28   PHOEBE: When asked of her hopes for the future, Castra
29   said she planned to be queen of a mid-Eastern country —
30   *any* mid-Eastern country. Either that or a shoe clerk at
31   *(Name of local store)*.

32   BEBEE: Her hobby is gumdrops.

33   PHOEBE: Castra's parents will graduate *next* year.

34   BEBEE: Well, there you have it.

35   PHOEBE: Our best bets for future fame and fortune.

1   BEBEE: And none of them came anywhere near the top of
2   their class.
3   PHOEBE: You look at them and wonder, is it really worth all
4   the time and effort to study hard, do your homework,
5   and get good marks? *(Girls look at each other and nod heads.)*
6   BEBEE and PHOEBE: You bet it is!
7
8
9
10
11
12
13
14
15
16
17
18
19
20
21
22
23
24
25
26
27
28
29
30
31
32
33
34
35

#37

Nursery Rhymes — Dreamville or Reality?

CAST: ANNOUNCER, male or female, On-Stage or Off; GIRL 1, shy, sweet, maybe even wearing a pinafore and bows on her shoes as she reads her part of the nursery rhymes; GIRL 2, dressed in up-to-date hip fashion as she reads the lines representing reality.

ANNOUNCER: Once again debate rages in education circles — do our old-fashioned nursery rhymes help or harm our youngsters?

  The Old School says the classic tales give children a great sense of security and allow emotionally helpful dream time.

  Nonsense, says the New Breed. The old-style rhymes will make us a nation of daydreamers, unable to cope with reality. They suggest a hard-line, tell-it-like-it-is approach. Let's give a listen.

GIRL 1:   *(She recites all rhymes sweetly.)* Humpty Dumpty sat on a wall, Humpty Dumpty had a great fall. All the king's horses and all the king's men . . .

GIRL 2:   *(Picking up rhyme in straightforward brusque style)* . . . drove right on by and why not? They didn't want to get involved. Know where I'm coming from?

GIRL 1:   Old King Cole was a merry old soul, a merry old soul was he. He called for his pipe, he called for his bowl, and he called for his fiddlers three.

GIRL: 2:   But one fiddler was smoking the king's pipe, another was sipping soup from his bowl and the third had a gig down in Nashville. Being a king is history. Monarchies are gone!

GIRL 1:   There was an old lady who lived in a shoe. She had so

1	many children she didn't know what to do . . .
2	GIRL 2: I'll tell you what she did. She hired a hotshot agent
3	and got on Phil, Oprah and Geraldo, telling her story and
4	plugging her book: "Nine Is Fine, but Twenty Is Plenty."
5	Now she and the gang are rich and they're living in a
6	luxury high-rise fisherman's boot in Malibu.
7	GIRL 1: Rub-a-dub, three men in a tub . . .
8	GIRL 2: I know there's a water shortage, but three bozos in a
9	tub? Strange stuff. I'm talking weird city.
10	GIRL 1: Diddle-diddle dumpling, my son John went to bed
11	with his stockings on. One shoe off and one shoe on . . .
12	GIRL 2: So? Something wrong? All teen-agers do that.
13	GIRL 1: Tom, Tom the piper's son, stole a pig and away he run.
14	GIRL 2: He would have gotten away, but his pig "squealed"
15	on him. *(Holds hand over eyes and shakes her head.)* Sorry,
16	folks. That slipped out. But that's what I get for
17	associating with this dream world crowd.
18	GIRL 1: Little Jack Horner sat in a corner, eating his pudding
19	and pie; he stuck in his thumb and pulled out a plum . . .
20	GIRL 2: *(Imitates her words. Puts thumb in imaginary pie, pulls it*
21	*out, looks at it, shakes head.)* Won't do much for his
22	hitchhiking.
23	GIRL 1: Hi-diddle-diddle, the cat and the fiddle, the cow
24	jumped over the moon . . .
25	GIRL 2: And the price of milk has been sky-high ever since.
26	Now, that's reality.
27	GIRL 1: Jack be nimble, Jack be quick, Jack jumped over the
28	candlestick . . .
29	GIRL 2: Now that definitely is *not* reality. I mean that's one
30	silly kid you got there. *(Shakes head and calls.)* Smarten
31	up, Jack.
32	GIRL 1: Wee Willie Winkie in his nightgown, early in the
33	morning would stroll through town . . .
34	GIRL 2: Sounds weird . . . but it kept him out of the Army for
35	three years.

1	GIRL 1:	Little Miss Muffet sat on a tuffet, eating her curds and
2		whey; along came a spider and sat down beside her ...
3	GIRL 2:	Hey, any girl who sits on a tuffet is gonna end up
4		with a spider next to her. And that snack! *(Grimaces)* Throw
5		that whey away.
6	GIRL 1:	There was a little girl who had a little curl *(Flips a*
7		*little bit of her hair onto her forehead)* right in the middle of
8		her forehead. When she was *(Big sweet smile)* good, she was
9		very, very good.
10	GIRL 2:	*(Jumping right in)* And when she was bad she was
11		popular. *(GIRL 1 is hurt; whirls on her.)*
12	GIRL 1:	That harsh type of talk gets you nowhere.
13	GIRL 2:	*(Taken aback)* Well ... I ... uh ...
14	GIRL 1:	Why don't you try a nice rhyme the old-fashioned
15		way, with meaning?
16	GIRL 2:	You mean like you've been doing? That stuff?
17	GIRL 1:	Yes. Go ahead. Try it. You'll like it.
18	GIRL 2:	I don't know any ... ah ... here's one ... The owl
19		*(Gestures to herself and then to GIRL 1)* and the pussycat went
20		to sea in a beautiful pea-green boat ...
21	GIRL 1:	*(With big smile)* See? Fine. But we'll ditch the pea-green
22		and make it royal blue and pink. And I'll have to get a
23		whole new sailing outfit ... *(She grabs reluctant friend by*
24		*the arm and starts marching her off, talking as she does so)*
25		... some heavy-soled deck shoes ... white yachting
26		cap ... I see a thirty-two-foot Chris Craft ...
27	GIRL 2:	*(Being led off)* Now that's reality.
28	GIRL 1:	*(Going on)* And we'll invite my sugar daddy for a cruise ...
29	GIRL 2:	*(To audience, defeated)* Now that's *real* reality!
30		
31		
32		
33		
34		
35		

#38

Wake Up! — Assert Yourself!

CAST: ANNOUNCER, male or female, On-Stage or Off; RUTH
and JOAN. Both performers are young, pleasant, attractive people.

SETTING: Desk or table with two chairs. Performers should be
seated. They have a book they refer to from time to time.

ANNOUNCER: **During the past few months there has been a
spate of books extolling individuality, self-assertiveness,
forceful extrovertism and personality recharging. In other
words, don't sit back and keep quiet — go out and express
yourself. Say what you think, anytime, anywhere. Let's
see what can happen.**

RUTH: *(To JOAN)* **I don't like what you did to me.**

JOAN: *(Defiantly)* **And I'd do it again tomorrow.** *(Pause)* **What
did I do to you?**

RUTH: *(Thinking)* **I don't know. Can't remember.**

JOAN: **But at least you spoke out. Don't you feel better about
yourself?**

RUTH: **I'm not sure. Maybe it won't work for me.**

JOAN: **Check the book. Try another one.**

RUTH: *(Checking book)* **Hey, friend, will you lend me twenty
dollars?**

JOAN: *(Puzzled)* **Who are you?**

RUTH: *(Uncertain)* **I don't know.**

JOAN: **Try again.**

RUTH: *(Refers to book.)* **Here's one you do on the job.**

JOAN: **Go ahead.**

RUTH: **Boss, on that last deal, I must say you are wrong.**

JOAN: **You are fired!** *(Closes book in dismay.)*

RUTH: **Not for me.**

1 JOAN: You think those are tough? Get a load of things you
2   should do if you *really* want to assert yourself, be
3   yourself, stand out in a crowd. *(She opens book and they*
4   *alternate reading the behavior actions to do for self-*
5   *assertiveness.)* Stick your tongue out at a mortician.
6 RUTH: *(Forcefully)* Wear a three-button blazer to a fireman's
7   picnic.
8 JOAN: *(Getting louder)* Challenge a one-legged man to a high
9   hurdles race.
10 RUTH: Put live ammunition in your nostrils and sneeze into
11   a crowd.
12 JOAN: Leave a welt on a perfect stranger.
13 RUTH: Grab a tall willowy girl by the ankles and snap her
14   like a whip.
15 JOAN: Take your date to a fancy restaurant and eat with
16   boxing gloves on.
17 RUTH: Too rough for me.
18 JOAN: They say if you do five of these things it will earn you
19   admiration and respect.
20 RUTH: Or at least a good rap in the mouth.
21 JOAN: You may be right.
22 RUTH: Let's just go back to being ourselves.
23 JOAN: Right. Just ourselves.
24 RUTH: *(After a pause)* Say, friend, will you lend me that
25   twenty dollars?
26 JOAN: *(Pauses, puzzled)* Who are you anyway?
27
28
29
30
31
32
33
34
35

39

What's Ahead in TV Land
for the Coming Season?

CAST: ANNOUNCER, male, On-Stage or Off; PATSY and PRUDENCE. Attractive, pleasant young women who take their jobs seriously. They are TV entertainment personalities.

SETTING: Table or desk with two chairs for the performers. Papers or notebooks from which the performers can read their lines. A mike set-up would help in the overall scene.

ANNOUNCER: **What's ahead for television viewers in the coming season? Will there be more specials, docu-dramas, quiz shows, sitcoms, soap operas, Westerns, cop shows? Well, here to tell you what's in store for all you video viewers out there are Patsy and Prudence, our two peerless prognasticators.**

PATSY: *(Calling with irritation from Off-Stage)* **What did you say?**

ANNOUNCER: *(Defending himself)* **Prognasticators. Look it up. It's clean.**

PRUDENCE: *(Moving On-Stage into position, along with PATSY)* **Wish we could say the same thing about you.** *(Girls sit down and pick up notes to read.)*

PATSY: **You want to start off our predictions for the coming TV season?**

PRUDENCE: **Why not? Here goes. On January tenth, there will be an hour-long special devoted entirely to TV newsmen. In it, Edwin S. Newman examines the first amendment, Sam Donaldson recites the letter "R," and in rapid-fire style, Harry Reasoner and Mike Wallace do an entire "60 Minutes" in three minutes and fourteen seconds, after which the entire group leaves for a**

1   pilgrimage to visit David Brinkley's birthplace.

2 PATSY: After complaints by numerous moral majority
3   groups, network executives, on the weekend of January
4   fourteenth, will announce there is to be no more out-and-
5   out sex and violence — performers will be limited to
6   committing minor indecencies.

7 PRUDENCE: January thirtieth — on "Star Search," strolling
8   swineherd Edgie Clendenon wins first prize by sticking
9   a pound of taffy in his mouth, pushing a wheelbarrow
10   and whistling "When My Sugar Walks Down the Street."

11 PATSY: February seventh — production halts on the set of
12   "Roseanne" when Roseanne's blouse explodes, injuring
13   five stagehands.

14 PRUDENCE: February nineteenth — when guests fail to
15   show up, Barbara Walters interviews herself, objects to
16   the questions and stalks off in a huff.

17 PATSY: March third — in an affirmative action move, Jack
18   Lord hires Chinese writer Ling Wong to script an
19   upcoming "Hawaii Five-O" episode.

20 PRUDENCE: March fourteenth — Don Rickles signs for
21   another television show of his own. No one knows what
22   it's about, but sponsors are rumored to be Scope, Right
23   Guard and Aqua Velva after shave.

24 PATSY: March thirtieth — Jack Lord fires Chinese writer
25   Ling Wong, claiming he put too much starch in his dialog.

26 PRUDENCE: April eighth — in full view of his audience,
27   diet and exercise guru, Richard Simmons collapses on
28   stage after OD-ing on health foods.

29 PATSY: April twentieth — during the filming of "Life Styles
30   of the Rich and Famous," Sean Penn becomes unruly in
31   a saloon and the bartender pours two warning shots over
32   his head.

33 PRUDENCE: May fifth — top TV newsmen leave to
34   accompany President Bush on his historic tour of the
35   Carlsbad Caverns.

1 PATSY: May twenty-eighth — Joan Collins signs to play a
2 swinging, lady-type person in "I Come from Alabama with
3 a Bagnio on My Knee."
4 PRUDENCE: June first — Richard Simmons, forty pounds
5 heavier, quits show and signs to play obese cop in next
6 three Sylvester Stallone movies.
7 PATSY: June tenth — top TV newsmen who covered the
8 President's trip to the Carlsbad Caverns admit
9 sheepishly it wasn't President Bush at all — it was
10 George Plimpton in a TV special.
11 PRUDENCE: *(Conversationally to PATSY)* And do we have
12 anything for our vast sports audience out there?
13 PATSY: You bet we do, Pru. On June twelfth — "Sports
14 World-Wide" makes its summer debut featuring the finals
15 in the Senior Citizens pole vault; a midget bullfight
16 starring "Stretch" Benson using a washcloth and needle
17 to fight a small wart hog, and Jacques Cousteau and his
18 new-found friend, Percy the Piranha, inspecting a giant
19 vat of tainted clam chowder.
20 PRUDENCE: July third — visiting French gourmet chef
21 guesting on Julia Child's show, drinks too much of the
22 cooking sherry and stuffs a turkey — into a pig's mouth.
23 PATSY: July twenty-first — featuring guest stars from
24 "General Hospital" and "Medical Center," CBS announces
25 a special called "The Bright Side of Depression."
26 PRUDENCE: July twenty-second — not to be outdone, ABC
27 announces that Dan Dierdorf, Frank Gifford and Al
28 Michaels will do a special called "Monday Night Medicine,"
29 with shows on psoriasis, rhinitis, elephantiasis, cirrhosis,
30 thrombosis, acidosis, halitosis and strange warts.
31 PATSY: August first — playwright Edward Albee relents
32 and agrees to write a TV drama. It centers on a love-
33 starved carpenter who pastes wood shavings on his head
34 to pass as curls so he can register at the YWCA.
35 PRUDENCE: September tenth — in the season's opener

1   against the Denver Broncos, rookie New York Giant
2   tight end Zinger Franzo makes television history by
3   catching a game-winning touchdown pass — and then
4   dropping it on the instant replay.
5 PATSY: September twenty-ninth — production on the
6   musical comedy version of "Ironsides" is delayed when
7   Raymond Burr is trapped atop the grease rack at the
8   studio garage.
9 PRUDENCE: October fourth — on a "Geraldo" show called
10   "Weirdos, USA," a self-confessed masochist reveals his
11   troubled past, saying he is giving it up and is down to
12   three smacks a day.
13 PATSY: October twenty-eighth — on "Night Court," Dan
14   Fielding prosecutes a man for transporting a bagpipe
15   across state lines for immoral purposes.
16 PRUDENCE: November third — "Eyewitness News" reports
17   on a tornado in Kansas and gets off eighteen witty
18   remarks — one for each victim.
19 PATSY: November eighteenth — in a remake of the Dorothy
20   Lamour film "Typhoon," under the new title, "Look what
21   They've Done to My Sarong, Ma," Bo Derek is trapped on
22   a tropical isle with a band of merry munchkins.
23 PRUDENCE: December fourth — angered by the defendant's
24   surly attitude, Judge Wapner sentences a pickpocket to
25   thirty days in the electric chair.
26 PATSY: December twenty-third — in an NBC holiday special,
27   famed Broadway Santa Claus Smiley Berdoo, is
28   pummeled by vandals disguised as elves and is stuffed
29   into his own Salvation Army collection pot as a chorus
30   of uniformed police come on the scene and sing "God
31   Arrest Ye Merry Gentlemen," for the first musical
32   mugging in TV history.
33 PRUDENCE: And that's the way your TV year will be.
34 ANNOUNCER: *(Off-Stage, calling out)* Thank you, girls.
35 PATSY: You're welcome, Sebastian.

1   **ANNOUNCER:**   What did you say?
2   **PRUDENCE:**   *(Calling out as girls prepare to leave)* **Look it up, it's**
3   **clean.** *(Girls exit, giggling happily.)*
4
5
6
7
8
9
10
11
12
13
14
15
16
17
18
19
20
21
22
23
24
25
26
27
28
29
30
31
32
33
34
35

#40

Movie Studio Auction

6 *CAST:* ANNOUNCER, male or female, On-Stage or Off; ANNIE
7 and AMANDA. They are bright, pleasant young women,
8 interested in doing their jobs well.

10 *SETTING:* Girls are seated at table or desk and have notebooks or
11 pads from which they can read their lines.

13 ANNOUNCER: **You've probably read about the auctions**
14 **conducted recently by major Hollywood studios, selling**
15 **their props to the highest bidders to raise much-needed**
16 **cash. Those were the big boys in the film business.**
17 **However, we've learned that a smaller studio, 19th**
18 **Century Wolf, is getting rid of its stocks to aid a**
19 **worthwhile charity — the Hollywood Home for the**
20 **Wayward Accordion Players. And who better to give us**
21 **a look at what's going on but Annie and Amanda, who**
22 **know what's happening in the world of make-believe.**
23 ANNIE: **Thank you, Sinclair** *(Shirley).* **I think this is a fine**
24 **thing that the studio is doing, don't you, Amanda?**
25 AMANDA: **I do indeed. People are so busy getting along in**
26 **this busy work-a-day world they forget just how many**
27 **wayward accordion players there are out there struggling**
28 **to get by.**
29 ANNIE: **They need all the help they can get. And we owe it to**
30 **them.**
31 AMANDA: **Right. Imagine never hearing "Lady of Spain"**
32 **again.**
33 ANNIE: **It would be an empty life. What are some of the items**
34 **the studio will auction off come next Monday?**
35 AMANDA: **For openers, they will sell the hospital bed used**

1   by Lionel Barrymore to treat a team of traveling midgets

2   suffering from bubonic plague in "Dr. Kildare Misplaces

3   His Nurse."

4 ANNIE: Loveseat used by Zsa Zsa Gabor during the filming

5   of "How Many Hearts Have I Broken?"

6 AMANDA: And then there's a candid photo of George Burns,

7   cigar in hand, crouching at a dressing room door as an

8   Indian maiden blows smoke signals through the keyhole.

9 ANNIE: *(Laughing)* I guess George got the message.

10 AMANDA: And there's a unique item — a statement of

11   import by Zasu Pitts printed on expensive palimpsest.

12 ANNIE: That should bring in big bucks. And then there's the

13   swamp Fred MacMurray stood in while portraying a

14   childless father in an episode of "Hey, I'm Lonely."

15 AMANDA: And there's Marlon Brando's undershirt from

16   "Streetcar Named Desire" with Kim Hunter's stand-in

17   still clinging to it.

18 ANNIE: Lots of good stuff. And how about this? A pair of

19   overalls once worn by Ma and Pa Kettle simultaneously.

20 AMANDA: And a cummerbund once worn by Raymond Burr

21   simultaneously.

22 ANNIE: That means money for those poor stomach Steinway

23   squeezers.

24 AMANDA: And how about this? A hitherto unreleased sixteen-

25   millimeter film documentary called "The Three Stooges

26   and Tuesday Weld Visit a Clinic."

27 ANNIE: I like this one. An action film showing John Wayne

28   forcing a water buffalo to crawl under a rocking chair.

29 AMANDA: An aerial photo of Raquel Welch picking up a

30   bucket of water in "100 Rifles" taken from the balcony of

31   Loew's 86th Street Theater.

32 ANNIE: Nostalgia buffs will go wild when these go on the

33   block.

34 AMANDA: You bet they will.

35 ANNIE: But if for some reason there are no takers, the studio

1	has offered — for the benefit of those accordion players
2	in mind — to let the whole package go — every item
3	mentioned here — for $187.48.
4	AMANDA: Slightly higher west of Dom DeLuise.
5	ANNIE: So get out there, you movie buffs, and help an
6	accordion player of your choice get on the right track.
7	AMANDA: Annie, did you ever go out with an accordion
8	player?
9	ANNIE: Yes ... *(Giggling)* he was my main squeeze. *(Curtain*
10	*or blackout)*
11	
12	
13	
14	
15	
16	
17	
18	
19	
20	
21	
22	
23	
24	
25	
26	
27	
28	
29	
30	
31	
32	
33	
34	
35	

#41

Truthsayer for the News

CAST: ANNOUNCER, male or female, On-Stage or Off; THERESA, bright, perky young lady who reads the news story with wide-eyed enthusiasm. She is in her early twenties; TRUDY, the truthsayer, a knowing, sardonic woman who explains the real facts behind the story. She can be any age.

SETTING: Desk with two chairs. Desk can have pads the girls can read from if they choose.

ANNOUNCER: **Lately a lot of doubt has been cast upon the credibility of our nation's media. Oh, not the kind of fabrication you see in headlines at supermarket checkouts. I mean just the regular day-to-day reporting of all kinds of stories. Some journalism experts have suggested broadcast stations and newspapers have a truthsayer to give the true facts to the public, the real story behind the story being presented. Let's see how this might work.**

THERESA: **Big story of the week in the social whirl was the wedding at Cheerful Chapel on Saturday.**

TRUDY: **That gives you some idea of the kind of week it was.**

THERESA: *(Reading)* **Cynthia Banderstand and Ed Slunk were married Saturday afternoon at the Cheerful Chapel by Parson Gustave Krile.**

TRUDY: **Great ceremony. You've heard of speed reading? The parson is a speed talker. It was over in twenty-six seconds.**

THERESA: **The bride is the daughter of Mr. and Mrs. Barley Benbownatookarooney.**

TRUDY: **What was it before they changed it?**

1   THERESA: They are very active in social circles.

2   TRUDY: The missus is a dirigible thief and the old man used
3   to take in laundry women.

4   THERESA: Mr. Benbownatookarooney is head of the city's
5   Wildlife Committee.

6   TRUDY: Saturday nights at the local country club.

7   THERESA: The bride's gown was of organza with a Venice
8   lace bodice and a lace-edged, chapel-length train.

9   TRUDY: One of the flower girls almost stepped on her
10   caboose.

11   THERESA: She wore a pearl brooch and carried a
12   handkerchief trimmed with sweetheart lace.

13   TRUDY: She wore the brooch up high to divert attention
14   away from her overbite. She's the only girl who can eat
15   corn on the cob through a picket fence.

16   THERESA: Her sister, Miss Margo Banderstand, was maid of
17   honor.

18   TRUDY: Calling Margo a maid of honor is like calling Jack
19   the Ripper a flirt.

20   THERESA: The groom is a consultant for the firm of Grosbeak
21   and Bludge.

22   TRUDY: He consults with the bosses as to what they will have
23   for lunch and then he brings it to them.

24   THERESA: The bride, a former model, plans to continue in
25   that field.

26   TRUDY: She models bicycle accessories.

27   THERESA: More than fifty guests enjoyed the reception at
28   the Goomore Inn.

29   TRUDY: Fifty guests out of five hundred ain't too much
30   enjoyment.

31   THERESA: After the affair, the couple left on a honeymoon
32   trip to the Nearby Mountains and Losers Lodge.

33   TRUDY: The groom had to be dragged kicking and screaming
34   to the train station while waving a large sign saying
35   *"help!"*

```
1    THERESA:   (To TRUDY) Now that didn't happen at all. I know.
2             Through the whole thing I kept out a close eye.
3    TRUDY:   It did happen. Remember, an eye for an eye and the
4             truth for the truth. (THERESA shakes her head vigorously
5             to audience, while TRUDY nods just as vigorously, smiling all
6             the time.)
7
8
9
10
11
12
13
14
15
16
17
18
19
20
21
22
23
24
25
26
27
28
29
30
31
32
33
34
35
```

#42

Love, Honor and Oh, Baby!

CAST: ANNOUNCER, male or female, On-Stage or Off; MAUD and MIRANDA, both pleasant and work well together. They can be any age.

SETTING: Desk or table and two chairs. Notebook or pad from which the performers can read their lines.

ANNOUNCER: The joys of wedded bliss often end up quickly with a good-by kiss. Yes, sad to say, what starts out to be a joyous union very often dissolves in anger and sadness. About half of all marriages performed in the United States these past few years have ended in divorce. Why? Let's ask our two merry mavens of matrimony — Maud and Miranda.

MAUD: Yes, no doubt about it, divorce is a sad thing.

MIRANDA: Before we investigate why people divorce we should first look into reasons people marry.

MAUD: Hopefully it's because they're in love, but often couples get married for rather strange reasons.

MIRANDA: Right. One young woman recently got married in the hopes that it would cure her hiccoughs.

MAUD: Sad. I know a young man who proposed marriage because he was tired of going to camp every summer.

MIRANDA: In a recent poll, they asked a puzzled and disgruntled man why he got married and he answered: "I don't know, we started out as friends."

MAUD: And today's marriages are of such brief duration. The other day a woman filed for divorce so fast, she got custody of the wedding cake.

MIRANDA: And the reasons for divorce certainly appear to

1   be whimsical and capricious in some cases.

2 MAUD: Right. I know of one woman who divorced her husband
3   because he clashed with the drapes.

4 MIRANDA: Another young lady got a divorce just to visit
5   Mexico.

6 MAUD: I think many of today's young marrieds are forgetting
7   their parents' teaching that divorce isn't something you
8   rush into.

9 MIRANDA: So true. One young bride filed for divorce
10   claiming her husband had failed to get a learner's permit
11   before taking out the license.

12 MAUD: I think there would be less divorce if young people
13   would take more time in choosing a mate. There are
14   warning signals. Your would-be mate could be all wrong
15   from the beginning.

16 MIRANDA: Right. For instance, a man should be wary of the
17   girl he is courting if she offers a free seven-day home trial.

18 MAUD: Or if he wants to elope and her parents offer to hold
19   the ladder.

20 MIRANDA: And what about women? They should be on guard
21   if he is about to take the premarital blood test and has
22   to send out for some.

23 MAUD: And a girl should be cautious if her intended refuses
24   to burn his membership card in the Lonely Hearts Club.

25 MIRANDA: Yes, there are precautions a wide-eyed, alert
26   person can take. It would certainly cut down on the
27   divorce rate.

28 MAUD: Yes, but if they do get married and they feel that
29   suddenly the bloom is off the rose, there *are* warning
30   signs.

31 MIRANDA: Right. These, if noted, give the couple time to
32   stand back and make a reassessment of their marriage.

33 MAUD: For instance, a marriage is in trouble when the
34   husband walks in his sleep and is carrying a suitcase.

35 MIRANDA: The marriage is in trouble when a wife takes the

1   tufts out of the electric toothbrush and puts in a hammer.
2   MAUD: When a husband has a hotline installed between his
3   bed and the YWCA.
4   MIRANDA: When there's moss growing on the love seat.
5   MAUD: When a wife throws her cigarette butt into the Grand
6   Canyon and asks her husband to step on it.
7   MIRANDA: When a husband receives a bouquet of forget-me-
8   nots from his wife.
9   MAUD: That's sad. But then the whole divorce issue is a sad
10   one.
11 MIRANDA: How true. But there are some sayings that might
12   help marrieds stay on track.
13 MAUD: Right. Marriages are like illnesses; you should only
14   have one at a time. The saddest man in the world is a
15   bigamist whose wives don't understand him.
16 MIRANDA: Men, tell your wife everything ... before she
17   reads about it.
18 MAUD: Here's a Confucious-type marital maxim — when
19   you put a woman on a pedestal, remember, it's easier for
20   her to kick you in the face.
21 MIRANDA: Life isn't all candlelight and money.
22 MAUD: Marriage is an educational institution. But why are
23   there so many dropouts?
24 MIRANDA: Marriage is habit-forming.
25 MAUD: Women are like books. When you marry, choose a
26   first edition rather than one from a circulating library.
27 MIRANDA: Good marriages make winters seem shorter.
28 MAUD: You should only be married once; but if you work it
29   right — (Seriously) once is enough.
30
31
32
33
34
35

#43

Hollywood Questions and Answers

CAST: ANNOUNCER, male or female, On-Stage or Off; MAUD and MATILDA, any age, who know all about Hollywood stars.

SETTING: Desk or table with two chairs from which the girls deliver their lines.

PROPS: Some small cards from which one girl can read the questions sent in by listeners.

ANNOUNCER: **America has long had a fascination for movies. They love to hear the inside stories of our favorites of the film world. Many of the country's cinema buffs write in to those in the industry for information about the performers. On hand today to answer questions from moviegoers are our two merry mavens of moviedom, Maud and Matilda.**

MAUD: **Thank you, Malcolm** *(Mary Jane).* **Are you ready for our first question, Matilda?**

MATILDA: **Question away, Maud.**

MAUD: *(Reads from card.)* **From Zanesville, Ohio — Twiggy was a famous model from England and made a movie or two. Whatever became of her?**

MATILDA: **Pencil-thin Twiggy is doing quite well, thank you. She works as a bookmark at a London lending library.**

MAUD: *(Reading)* **I hear stories that Dolly Parton is really Siamese twins. Is that true?**

MATILDA: **Despite many rumors to the contrary, Dolly Parton is really one person — she's joined at the hip.**

MAUD: *(Reading from card)* **Jill St. John was the talk of a recent Hollywood party. What was the costume she wore?**

MATILDA: **A double-breasted loincloth and hot pants with**

1   directional signals.

2 MAUD: *(Reading)* What is the latest information on Jane
3   Fonda?

4 MATILDA: She is involved in numerous social causes, including
5   fighting for the rights of shorter-than-average plumbers.
6   She also is spearheading the move to allow weaning
7   lobsters in distress.

8 MAUD: *(Reading)* Tell me what Tuesday Weld is up to.

9 MATILDA: Tuesday is busy doing aerobics for a fee, likes
10   English muffins and sleeps only in the upper part of her
11   pajama bottoms. She recently changed her name to
12   Wednesday.

13 MAUD: *(Reading)* I recently saw a rerun of "The Godfather."
14   How did they get Marlon Brando to look so fat and jowly?

15 MATILDA: Sheer Hollywood magic. They stuffed a live
16   squirrel in each of his cheeks.

17 MAUD: *(Reading)* Is Dustin Hoffman really a midget?

18 MATILDA: How absurd! Of course not. You're thinking of
19   Clint Eastwood who is really only three-feet-six.

20 MAUD: *(Reading)* What caused the latest oil slick off Los
21   Angeles that held up production on several Hollywood
22   films?

23 MATILDA: It puzzled authorities for a while until they
24   discovered it was started when Ricardo Montalban fell
25   off his yacht in Santa Monica Bay.

26 MAUD: Is it true that Shelley Winters had to gain fifty pounds
27   for her role in a recent movie?

28 MATILDA: Yes, and she did a great job. In addition, while
29   still carrying the weight, she has signed for a new film
30   in which she will dress in a Matterhorn suit and appear
31   as an Alp.

32 MAUD: Actress Meryl Streep reportedly has a new love in
33   her life. Can you tell us about this?

34 MATILDA: Meryl Streep has many friends, but for what it's
35   worth, she recently built a new home in Hollywood and

1   installed a swimming pool shaped like Raymond Burr.

2 MAUD: "Last Tango in Paris" came to cable TV and I wonder
3   how they got Marlon Brando to look so bulky and
4   overweight?

5 MATILDA: They stuffed live squirrels in his raincoat pockets.

6 MAUD: What was Farley Granger's first job in Hollywood?

7 MATILDA: Farley started humbly. His first job in Movieland
8   was stuffing starlets into sweaters for MGM.

9 MAUD: Is Vanessa Redgrave doing any film work right now?

10 MATILDA: She recently completed "Oh, Oh, Odalisque" in
11   which she stunned the blasé Hollywood crowd with a
12   sizzling bit of Terpsichore called "The Dance of the Seven
13   Travails."

14 MAUD: How did Zsa Zsa Gabor do on her latest divorce
15   settlement?

16 MATILDA: Great. She obtained visiting rights to her ex's
17   diamond mines weekends and holidays and received full
18   custody of their three swimming pools — Jeffrey, fifteen
19   feet deep; Lynn, twelve feet and Nicky, six feet deep.

20 MAUD: Could you tell me how Burt Reynolds keeps his hair
21   so wavy?

22 MATILDA: Burt has straight hair. It's his head that's wavy.

23 ANNOUNCER: *(On-Stage or Off)* Well, that's about it, girls.
24   Thank you very much for that bit of inside Hollywood.

25 MAUD: Until next time, Malcolm *(Mary Jane)*. *(Girls get up*
26   *together and head off, chatting amiably.)* Is it true what they
27   say about . . . *(Whispers to MATILDA)*

28 MATILDA: That's what I hear. And let me tell you about . . .
29   *(Leans over and whispers to MAUD)* They say . . . *(More*
30   *whispering)*

31 MAUD: Wow! And how about . . . *(She whispers again as they*
32   *exit)*

33 MATILDA: That's the story, Maud. And did you hear about . . .
34   *(More whispering as they exit)*

35

#44

Today's TV Telephone Talk Time

CAST: ANNOUNCER, male or female, On-Stage or Off; BECKY, a woman in her late twenties or early thirties. She is a no-nonsense operator of a telephone answering service; BUNNY, a younger, eager job aspirant in her first day on the job at the firm of Today's TV Telephone Talk Time.

SETTING: Table with four or five telephones, numerous pads and pencils. Two chairs are near the table. Girls can alternately sit and stand as they deliver their lines.

ANNOUNCER: **If you watch much television, you know the commercial breaks between programs are filled these days with telephone numbers to call. Viewers are invited to call up and talk to people about their problems, or hear confessions from real live people, or talk to wrestlers. Call a lawyer if you've got problems, or call and listen to a celebrity, or hopefully meet a member of the opposite sex in the hopes of developing a meaningful relationship. Children are advised not to call these programs without consulting their parents first. Who would call programs like this and pay up to two dollars a minute? Somebody must be calling, because television advertising costs a pretty penny. I can't imagine who would call any of these numbers. On the other hand, who are the people who answer? Let's check in with Today's TV Telephone Talk Time.**

(OPENING: BECKY is talking on the telephone at the table.)

BECKY: **Yes, sir, and I hope you're feeling better. Thanks for calling.** *(Hangs up phone. BUNNY walks in, smiling and bubbly. It is her first day on the job and she is eager to get to*

1	*work. BECKY holds out her hand and greets her in friendly*
2	*fashion.)* **You're Bunny. Welcome aboard.**
3	BUNNY: **Thank you, Miss Jones.**
4	BECKY: **Becky. Everyone here is on first name basis only.**
5	**Company policy in all our branches.**
6	BUNNY: *(Happily)* **That's nice. Makes it so much more friendly.**
7	BECKY: **Right. Now briefly, here's what you'll be doing. We**
8	**have a whole bank of phones here. We offer all sorts of**
9	**services. Listening to tales of woe, taking calls from the**
10	**lonely, from wrestling fans, people who need lawyers,**
11	**people who need help in slimming down or remolding**
12	**their figures, callers who want to meet a friend with a**
13	**nice voice.**
14	BUNNY: *(Puzzled)* **But where are the other people for all those**
15	**categories?**
16	BECKY: *(Smiles, pointing a finger at BUNNY and then herself.)*
17	**You and me.**
18	BUNNY: **Just us? On all those phones?**
19	BECKY: **Right. You just have to have some knowledge in lots**
20	**of areas and be sympathetic.** *(Phone rings.)* **Watch me.**
21	*(Picks up phone, checks which phone service it is.)* **Shoppers**
22	**Saving.** *(Listens)* **Yes ... isn't that a lovely choker? I'm**
23	**wearing one myself.** *(She isn't. She looks at BUNNY and*
24	*shrugs.)* **Right ... Only nineteen ninety-five with the old**
25	**one. You can wear it anywhere.** *(Listens)* **Certainly, even**
26	**bullfights. Or fly casting events.** *(Nodding)* **Map folding**
27	**contest. Right. Anywhere.** *(BUNNY looks on admiringly.)*
28	**Just send in your money to the address on the screen.**
29	**Right. Thank you, sir.** *(Hangs up phone.)*
30	BUNNY: *(Admiringly)* **Boy, that's great.**
31	BECKY: **It's easy, once you get the hang of it. Just make sure**
32	**you know which phone you're answering.**
33	BUNNY: **Right.** *(A phone rings.)*
34	BECKY: *(Points to a phone.)* **You take it.**
35	BUNNY: *(After a pause, picks up a phone.)* **Have a Date, Meet a**

1	Mate. *(Listens)* **You'd like to have a date and meet a mate?**
2	**Precisely why we're here.** *(Listens)* **Why, thank you. You**
3	**have a nice voice too.** *(Listens)* **Me? Tomorrow night? No,**
4	**sorry, sir. We don't provide those services. What we do**
5	**is listen to the type of girl you have in mind and then**
6	**provide a list of ladies who meet those qualifications. You**
7	**call them, and after that you're on your own. What kind**
8	**of girl are you interested in?** *(Listens)* **Wow! I don't think**
9	**we have anybody like that on our list!** *(She looks at BECKY*
10	*and holds hand to her forehead.)* **I'll check it out. Send in**
11	**your name, address and phone number to the address on**
12	**the screen and you're on your way. Thank you for calling**
13	**Have a Date.** *(Hangs up phone. To BECKY)* **Boy, he has high**
14	**hopes, I must say.** *(Phone rings; BECKY picks up a phone.)*
15	BECKY: *(Deep voice)* **Women in Wrestling.** *(Listens)* **What?**
16	**That's very interesting. You're going to marry Betty the**
17	**Bayonne Bouncer? Congratulations. And what do you**
18	**do?** *(Listens)* **You're a wrestler too? Two wrestlers**
19	**marrying. Hope you enjoy the state of holy headlock.**
20	**Many happy airplane spins and body slams. Thank you**
21	**for calling.** *(BECKY hangs up phone. Another one rings.*
22	*BECKY points to BUNNY and to phone. BUNNY picks it up*
23	*after checking which phone it is.)*
24	BUNNY: *(Into phone)* **Legalized Lawyers Limited. Yes, sir.**
25	*(Listens)* **You want a divorce. Why?** *(Listens and repeats.)*
26	**You're a masochist. You like getting pummeled.** *(Looks at*
27	*BECKY, shakes head and listens.)* **Your wife is a sadist. Does**
28	**she beat you up?** *(Listens)* **She *doesn't* beat you up. She's**
29	**nice to you and it's driving you crazy and you want to**
30	**leave. Yes, I guess you could charge breach of brutality.**
31	*(Listens)* **No, I don't think it constitutes a felony.** *(Listens)*
32	**What?! What did you call me?** *(Listens)* **Oh . . . a tort. Yes,**
33	**it could be classified as a tort. Hope we've been of some**
34	**help. Thanks for calling.** *(To BECKY)* **Had a bad connection.**
35	*(Phone rings; BECKY answers.)*

1   BECKY: Hello, General Information. No . . . this isn't police
2   emergency nine-one-one. That's all right. *(Hangs up. Phone*
3   *rings; BUNNY picks it up.)*
4   BUNNY: General Information. *(Listens)* Yes, we are active in
5   show business. What do you do? *(Listens)* You give
6   imitations of fireworks displays? Sounds interesting.
7   *(Listens)* On radio? Golly, sir, I don't think there's much
8   call for that. But thanks for calling. Keep trying. *(Listens,*
9   *shakes head.)* Hey, you're good. That's Fourth of July if I
10   ever heard it. Keep on trying. *(Hangs up. Phone rings;*
11   *BECKY gets this one.)*
12   BECKY: *(Into phone)* Trim and Slim for Her and Him. *(Listens,*
13   *repeats.)* Do I know any method to increase the size of
14   your upper torso? Yes, miss, I do. Here's what you do.
15   *(She gestures to BUNNY to follow her directions. BUNNY gets*
16   *it, nods.)* Hold your arms far out in front of you. Place
17   your fingertips together. Press hard. Then relax. *(She looks*
18   *at BUNNY who is following her directions.)* Press hard. Relax.
19   Do this for three minutes five times a day. It will increase
20   your measurements. *(Listens)* Of course it will work. My
21   friend tried it. Worked perfectly. She added three
22   inches . . . to her fingers. *(She hangs up phone. Both girls*
23   *begin giggling.)* Oh, that was awful of me. Just couldn't
24   resist. Not very professional. *(Phone rings.)* You take it,
25   Bunny.
26   BUNNY: *(Into phone)* You'll Never Be Lonely with Your One
27   and Only. *(Listens; is shocked.)* Hey, fella, cut that out!
28   *(Listens)* Oh . . . you have asthma. Sorry. *(Listens)*
29   No . . . this isn't police emergency nine-one-one. *(Hangs*
30   *up phone. Phone rings; BECKY grabs it.)*
31   BECKY: *(Into phone)* Happy Horoscope. No, this isn't police
32   emergency nine-one-one. *(Hangs up phone. Shakes head.)*
33   Boy, there's lots of trouble out there.
34   BUNNY: *(Phone rings; BUNNY into phone)* You'll Never Be
35   Lonely with Your One and Only. *(Listens)* A date. *(Repeats)*

1	Tall, redhead, a shape that doesn't quit, legs that come
2	all the way up, intellectual, great conversationalist,
3	witty, stylish dresser. Sir, I think you're talking about
4	four different girls. Do you have trouble getting dates?
5	What do you look like? *(Listens)* Six feet tall. Brown wavy
6	hair. Fair complexion. Good build. *(At this, BECKY looks*
7	*over questioningly, with interest.)* Say, your voice sounds
8	familiar. Are you a singer? It's so familiar. Say, is your
9	name Joe? No. Fred. *(BECKY is interested. She pic¹ s up*
10	*another phone and listens in.)* Fred, are you a public speaker?
11	No. You sound just like a guy I'm dating.
12	BECKY: *(Interrupting)* You sound just like a guy I'm dating.
13	Are you Arnold?
14	BUNNY: *(To BECKY)* It's Fred.
15	BECKY: Sounds like Arnold. OK . . . Fred . . . if that's your
16	name . . . say "rubber, buggy, bumper" fast three times.
17	*(Both girls are listening. BECKY shouts.)* You're Arnold!
18	BUNNY: Sounds like Joe. Do you know a girl named Bunny?
19	BECKY: No, but your Fred/Joe knows a Becky! Arnold, I'll
20	see you tomorrow at eight. *(She hangs up.)*
21	BUNNY: *(Into phone)* Joe . . . Saturday at seven. *(She hangs*
22	*up. Girls face each other.)*
23	BECKY: How dare you come in here and try to steal my boy
24	friend?!
25	BUNNY: *Your* boy friend? I've known him for four months!
26	BECKY: Me — six months! I knew him first.
27	BUNNY: But he likes me better. I'm younger.
28	BECKY: What?! *(Phone rings. BECKY grabs it quickly. Angrily)*
29	Yeah. *(Listens)* No, this isn't police emergency nine-one-
30	one . . . *(Glares at BUNNY)* . . . but we may be calling the
31	*police* and *hospital* emergency pretty soon. *(She slams*
32	*down phone. The two girls face each other and begin raucous*
33	*ad-lib name calling, threatening, going head to head and toe to*
34	*toe with each other at the curtain or blackout.)*
35	

#45

Some Expert Help for the
Non-Too-Frequent Traveler

CAST: ANNOUNCER, male or female, On-Stage or Off; AMELIA, pleasant assistant to Dr. Flightly; DR. FLIGHTLY, older woman who seems to know everything about travel. Has a tendency to ramble on with her answers. If desired, she can wear some sort of travel gear, helmet, long scarf, etc.

SETTING: Desk or table with two chairs. Performers can sit or stand.

ANNOUNCER: People who travel often return home tired or dispirited. Why? Because they've made some mistakes along the way. In foreign countries, Americans seem to blunder with regards to the currency exchange or local customs. Fortunately for you, infrequent travelers, we have with us the famed Dr. Eleanor Flightly, journey consultant extraordinaire, who will help out by solving the questions asked most often by travelers who erred along the way. With her is her assistant, Amelia.

AMELIA: Thank you. And now, Doctor, are you ready to answer the questions from travelers in trouble?

DOCTOR: Clear the decks. I'm ready for action and to help out all those people who go places but don't know what they're doing and why they do it.

AMELIA: OK, Doctor, here is question number one. When should you never switch from one airline to another?

DOCTOR: When the plane is in flight. That is a no-no. It can be hazardous to your health and maybe upset a few of the passengers on board.

AMELIA: What's the riskiest thing you can do in booking a

1   Caribbean yacht charter?

2 DOCTOR: Riskiest thing you can do *is* booking a Caribbean

3   yacht charter. Don't you read the papers? Trouble.

4   Explosions. People hurting each other. Do what I do. Stop

5   reading the papers.

6 AMELIA: OK, Doctor. What's the most expensive mistake

7   most travelers make in Hong Kong?

8 DOCTOR: Going to Hong Kong is the most expensive

9   mistake. But if you've got the loot, go ahead, take a ‹ hot.

10   But behave. None of those easy intermarriage jokes like

11   "two Wongs don't make a white." They don't like that

12   over there. I'm not crazy about them either if the truth

13   be known.

14 AMELIA: Why should you be careful about shipping things

15   back from Africa?

16 DOCTOR: Things from Africa have a tendency to escape and

17   run riot. A friend of mine recently sent a pygmy and

18   didn't pack him properly. And if you don't pack a pygmy

19   properly you are asking for trouble. They sneak around

20   all over the place and with those darts . . . I'm talking riot

21   conditions.

22 AMELIA: So you advise travelers to pack pygmies properly?

23 DOCTOR: You catch on fast. That's the story.

24 AMELIA: If an airline cancels your flight and tries to put you

25   on one several hours later, what's the first thing you

26   should do?

27 DOCTOR: Throw a tantrum. Lie down on the floor in the

28   terminal, kick your feet and shout dire imprecations to

29   the airlines in general and to the booking clerk in

30   particular.

31 AMELIA: A tantrum?

32 DOCTOR: Exactly. Like this. *(Drops to the floor and carries on in*

33   *a wild manner, then stands up, the picture of dignity.)*

34 AMELIA: That's a real tantrum.

35 DOCTOR: Hey, I've had enough experience. Do it all the time.

1   Never fails. If you can't do a tantrum, a little fit will
2   suffice.
3   AMELIA: What basic rule should experienced travelers
4   observe before checking in their luggage on a flight?
5   DOCTOR: Listen closely. If you hear ticking in some other
6   luggage, don't check it in — check out, fast! Take a cab.
7   Hit the bricks. Vamoose hurriedly.
8   AMELIA: Make an exit.
9   DOCTOR: Couldn't have said it better myself.
10   AMELIA: In flying from the U.S. to Australia, what's the worst
11   mistake you can make?
12   DOCTOR: Flying outside the plane just to save a few dollars.
13   That's a big mistake. You can get a head cold and you
14   get high-flying bugs in your teeth. Get inside the plane,
15   get a seat and doze off. Pretty soon your in Australia and
16   so what? With all those boxing kangaroos and aborigines
17   and stuff. What good did it do you? And who's gonna
18   listen to you when you get back? Not me, that's for sure.
19   AMELIA: Thank you, Doctor Flightly. I'm off to Disneyland
20   for two weeks. How about you?
21   DOCTOR: *(Starts rambling.)* Home base. My backyard. Make
22   some ham salad sandwiches, big pitcher of iced tea,
23   sprinkle a few ants around and have a picnic. Can't stand
24   those noisy travelers who go to Hong Kong and Africa
25   and send me gifts. Tell you, nobody seems to know how
26   to pack a pygmy properly. They get out and run around
27   the yard with those darts and stuff . . . I tell you . . .
28   AMELIA: *(Courteously as she lets her ramble)* Thank you, Doctor
29   Flightly, enjoy your rest . . . take a long, long rest . . .
30
31
32
33
34
35

OPTIONAL

#46

Writers — Stay Home and Make Big Money

CAST: ANNOUNCER, male or female, On-Stage or Off; Two members of the Society of Literary American Booksellers, SLABS ONE and TWO, male or female.

ANNOUNCER: If you're troubled with insomnia, just turn on a talk show with an author out there plugging his book. Guaranteed you'll be snoozing in minutes.

No doubt about it, authors don't sparkle on the tube, with an occasional exception. On a charisma scale of one to ten, authors usually average minus four. This does not sell books.

But an enterprising outfit called the Society of Literary American Booksellers — SLABS — has come on to the scene to hype book sales. They hire bright-eyed, bubbling, animated actors and actresses to fill in for the true authors, pretending they are the writers, most of whose faces are unknown to the viewing public.

Here now are two members of SLABS to tell you all about their operation.

SLAB ONE: Yes, we do look for personality people to pose as authors.

SLAB TWO: We have our latest casting list ready for you perky performers out there.

SLAB ONE: Your chance, boys and girls, to pose as prosaic authors and make good money doing it.

SLAB TWO: Build up your resumé with TV credits — and make good money doing it.

SLAB ONE: Here are the people we're looking forward to to pose as writers and make good money doing it.

SLAB TWO: Wanted — actress, about thirty, hopefully with

1   exophthalmos — make that bulging eyeballs — to match
2   tone of book entitled "Make Power Blackouts Work for
3   You."
4   A "Directory for the Ambitious" is the subtitle of
5   this profusely illustrated volume which tells how to make
6   extra cash during the next power blackout.
7   Author tells how to make glow-in-the-dark wheelchairs
8   to prevent corridor collisions and sell trained glowworms
9   to stuff into nudists' navels when your utility company
10   fails again.
11 SLAB ONE: Wanted — actor, unattractive, morose, a loser,
12   to pose as author of "Eight Clubs to Join."
13   There are 49,457 different clubs in America and
14   they're all listed here in no particular order as the author
15   tries heroically to, quote — "make loneliness obsolete,"
16   end quote.
17   Eight clubs need members badly and they're all
18   detailed — National Association of Starfish Gazers,
19   Hermits Unlimited, Ancient Order of Hermaphrodites,
20   Sloppy People, USA, John Dillinger Fan Club, Chasm
21   Inspectors, Slap and Tell Association and Tango Dancers
22   without Partners. A fine assignment for a fine actor.
23 SLAB TWO: Wanted — actor with open face, ingenuous,
24   child-like — stupid looking. The book is called "How to
25   Jack Up Your Car's Worth for Resale."
26   For the many motorists who've been stuck by used
27   car salesmen, here is the definitive handbook which tells
28   how to get your car in apparent tiptop shape so you can
29   stick some other sucker.
30   Schematic instructions show how to fake installation
31   of four-wheel brakes using cotton candy, use eiderdown
32   pillows instead of authentic shock absorbers and cross
33   wires in your odometer cable so the mileage goes down
34   as you drive. If purchased before Christmas, publishers
35   will include at no extra charge a statuette of Ralph Nader

1   for your dashboard.

2   Yes, actors, here's your chance to help America's fall
3   guys and dolls not get mad, but get even.

4 SLAB ONE: Wanted — burly actor, athletically inclined with
5   good hands who can go to his right and show great lateral
6   pursuit to fill role as author of "The Boston Strangler's
7   Physical Fitness Program."

8   Profusely illustrated with actual line drawings of
9   the famed Beantown Bad Boy in action, this fast-paced
10   treatise tells male readers how they can acquire dynamic
11   tension and lasting good health by following his rules.
12   Secret techniques of stalking, pouncing, leaping,
13   grabbing and holding to increase physical strength and
14   agility are handled deftly and specifically, yet with good
15   taste.

16   "How to Revitalize Your Chest While Wearing a
17   Body Shirt" and "Pardon Me, Ma'am" are two of the
18   liveliest chapters.

19   All you rugged males out there, this is the role for
20   you. So, give us a call at the SLABS casting office in Times
21   Square. Sign up with us.

22 SLAB TWO: And when people ask what you are, you can
23   proudly say:

24 SLAB ONE and TWO: I am a SLAB.

25

26

27

28

29

30

31

32

33

34

35

#47

It's All in the Mind

CAST: ANNOUNCER, male or female, On-Stage or Off; Two Pitch Persons, referred to as ONE and TWO in the sketch, male or female. Aggressive, forceful and experienced in what they do.

SETTING: Table with some papers on it. The sales duo can stand and occasionally refer to or pick up a paper to read from.

ANNOUNCER: **Psychiatry has long been a fashionable buzz word tossed about at parties, on buses, airports — anywhere people gather. But who knows what psychiatry really is?**

The father of psychiatry is Sigmund Freud, known to people in the know as "Big Daddy." Freud stated that the human personality consists of three parts — the Id, the Ego and the Super Ego. But what are they?

The Id is the unconscious — the part of the mind that lives by dreams and images. The Ego lives in the real world and tries to make the Id's dreams come true. The Super Ego is the *head honcho*, the *big guy*, the *boss* who tries to keep things running smoothly in keeping with the general norms of the community.

As we all know, occasionally things go wrong with one or more of these parts. So what do we do? We replace them at places like the Piece of Our Minds Used Parts Paradise.

ONE: **Ladies and gentlemen, perhaps you've been wanting to change your Id...**

TWO: **Your unconscious.**

ONE: **Or your Ego...**

TWO: **That's your conscious factor.**

1 ONE: ...but are confused with the mystifying ads of
2   personality component hucksters.
3 TWO: Well, we lay our cards right on the table. If you don't
4   need a new Id, we won't sell you one.
5 ONE: And seriously, folks, have you checked the lining on
6   your Id recently?
7 TWO: When was the last time you stemmed an aggressive
8   impulse without having feelings of penitence?
9 ONE: Does your Super Ego measure up?
10 TWO: We have them all here.
11 ONE: Let us tell you what we have in stock.
12 TWO: For instance, we have a practically new Id that has
13   gone only twenty-three thousand wish fulfillments.
14 ONE: Plenty of use left in this baby. Has new sidewalls and a
15   new impulse tabulator.
16 TWO: Just two hundred thirty dollars with the old one.
17 ONE: One of our big bargains is a practically new Id which
18   was traded in to us by a sixteen-year-old girl who had
19   never been kissed.
20 TWO: Original motor.
21 ONE: Comes equipped with a self-starting pleasure principle.
22 TWO: Only three hundred dollars.
23 ONE: Need a new Ego? We have one that came to us from a
24   school teacher who used it only on Sundays.
25 TWO: Thoroughly unfulfilled and just right for a young,
26   ambitious, rising executive who wants to get ahead but
27   isn't quite ruthless enough.
28 ONE: And this month's Mechanic's Special — a rebuilt Ego,
29   taken from a purse snatcher who used it to and from
30   work for eleven years.
31 TWO: It has been overhauled and there's still plenty of go,
32   go, go in this number. Secondary process has been
33   reconditioned.
34 ONE: Good transportation — seventy-five dollars.
35 TWO: And, naturally, you'll want to know about our famous

1		selection of name-brand Super Egos, if you really want
2		to change your life!
3	ONE:	Rows upon rows of Super Egos hanging from plain gas
4		pipe racks.
5	TWO:	Super Egos that have hardly even been used. Practically
6		never!
7	ONE:	Your choice from such famous Super Egos as Adolph
8		Hitler.
9	TWO:	Joseph Stalin.
10	ONE:	Al Capone.
11	TWO:	Attila the Hun.
12	ONE:	John Dillinger.
13	TWO:	And for that young couple in love — Bonnie and Clyde.
14	ONE:	All in fine working condition.
15	TWO:	Only the best in our Super Ego department.
16	ONE:	Come into any of our convenient downtown locations
17		or at the mall and walk out twenty minutes later with a
18		neat, well-fitting, smart-looking Super Ego that will
19		amaze your friends. You want something? Now you can
20		go out and get it!
21	TWO:	When purchasing these name-brand Super Egos we
22		must insist on cash payment.
23	ONE:	In advance!
24	TWO:	Matter of company policy.
25	ONE:	Naturally, we stand behind all our products.
26	TWO:	We give you a full thirty-day guarantee on any used Id,
27		Ego or Super Ego.
28	ONE:	And to those of you good people out there who buy a
29		Super Ego — say Mussolini's or Fidel Castro's — you
30		might find you'll have some difficulty in getting adjusted
31		to life with your new outlook.
32	TWO:	Well, just rest easy. You'll be reassured to know that
33		we have a whole stable full of competent psychiatrists
34		who will be ready and willing to testify on your behalf
35		if and when you get arrested and end up in court.

1   ONE: But don't worry about that now.

2   TWO: Right. Come in, look around, pick out something you

3   like and walk out a new, restyled, remodeled human

4   being.

5   ONE: Thank you.

6

7

8

9

10

11

12

13

14

15

16

17

18

19

20

21

22

23

24

25

26

27

28

29

30

31

32

33

34

35

#48

At Last — Payoffs for Crime Victims

CAST: ANNOUNCER, male or female, On-Stage or Off; Two Pitch Persons, referred to as ONE and TWO in the sketch. Preferably male, but females would be all right.

SETTING: None required.

PROPS: Two posters held by speakers.

ANNOUNCER: At long last, several states have come up with plans to compensate mugging and hold-up victims with financial remuneration commensurate with the damages inflicted. How does it work right here in our state? Let's find out.

(OPENING: ONE and TWO walk out, each holding a poster to which they'll refer occasionally as they speak.)

ONE: Yes, folks, all you past, present and future victims of criminal physical attacks can be compensated for your troubles.

TWO: You're entitled to money regardless of your race, creed or color.

ONE: If you receive a simple bruise or laceration you receive ninety-five cents.

TWO: A broken digit is worth a dollar eighty . . . a black eye, two dollars.

ONE: Abdominal pummeling — resulting in loss of appetite or "Sluggee's Disease," wherein victim suddenly doubles over in pain *(Demonstrates)* when confronted by a stranger — fourteen dollars and seventy-five cents!

TWO: Broken arm — fifteen dollars.

ONE: Broken jaw — twenty-seven dollars and fifty cents.

TWO: Internal injuries — proof required — thirty-one dollars.

1   ONE: Multiple wounds due to persistent bludgeoning —
2   eighty dollars.

ONE: Multiple wounds due to persistent bludgeoning — eighty dollars.

TWO: Thorough maiming — eighty-two dollars and thirty-nine cents.

ONE: Simple death — one hundred ninety dollars and five cents — the big bundle.

TWO: A little advice about the rules for all you attackees out there: application for payments must be made within ten days after the attack.

ONE: Or five days before death — whichever occurs first.

TWO: Note the pricing structure. *(Holds up chart.)* A black eye brings two dollars, while a broken jaw is worth twenty-seven fifty.

ONE: A simple taunt or mild insult might enrage even the most experienced hood and cause him to add injuries to your list, hoisting you into the high-money category.

TWO: It's possible he might even kick you while you're down and break a few ribs which goes for thirty dollars a copy.

ONE: However, you must not *request* that he injure you severely, as this is in violation of the Code, Article 3, Section 5.

TWO: Should you be subjected to a second attack, the compensation is increased by twenty per cent.

ONE: A third job means a hike of another forty per cent.

TWO: No one victim will be paid for more than three beatings within an eight-month period.

ONE: All payments are guaranteed by the Bleeding Heart and Vital Organs Insurance Company.

TWO: Just a word of caution to all of you out there.

ONE: Remember, some of the criminals out there are said by some to be emotionally distraught, victims of a callous society.

TWO: When he asks you for your money, he's really asking for help.

1   ONE: But please play it safe — give him your money.
2   TWO: You'll be glad you did.
3
4
5
6
7
8
9
10
11
12
13
14
15
16
17
18
19
20
21
22
23
24
25
26
27
28
29
30
31
32
33
34
35

#49

Take Me to a Leader — Any Leader

CAST: ANNOUNCER, male or female, On-Stage or Off; WIFFY, male or female; WACKY, male or female.

SETTING: Desk or table with two chairs.

PROPS: Far-out drawings or photos, possibly representing the characters described by the two performers. Though preferred, the graphics aren't really necessary. But if they are bizarre enough, they could get good laughs between the bits of dialog.

ANNOUNCER: Students, why be left out in the cold? Looking for a good protest group to join but can't find the right one? Well, don't fret any longer. Our two protest experts have singled out several top leaders for you to follow. Why grope around your high school or college corridors alone, seeking a leader to guide you in protesting? Pick a leader. And follow. Here are Wiffy and Wacky.

WIFFY: For openers we have . . .

WACKY: Glabby Scofflad. *(Holds up picture.)*

WIFFY: Glabby is most famous for his efforts to legalize contraband substances.

WACKY: He's fought to make them mandatory for people over sixteen.

WIFFY: An inspirational leader of the Militant Modern Meteorologists, he lights a fire under his charges by throwing hand grenades down the backs of their pants.

WACKY: True, he occasionally loses a member — or parts of one — but the impact usually brings great publicity and several others into the fold.

WIFFY: His group is also committed to total withdrawal of troops from high schools and sauna baths.

1	WACKY:	Right now the group numbers five hundred strong
2		— and six hundred weak.
3	WIFFY:	Glabby feels terrorizing sexagenarians, snatching
4		purses from wheelchair riders is where it's at right now.
5	WACKY:	Always selective, Glabby is against subway rioting,
6		feeling that is only token violence.
7	WIFFY:	His stomach protrudes.
8	WACKY:	*(Holding up picture)* Perry Bobbin.
9	WIFFY:	"Old Lavender and Lace" is a gritty, in-slapper from
10		way back.
11	WACKY:	One of the best known of the new leaders.
12	WIFFY:	He became a martyr for the cause when he was
13		incarcerated for hitting a policeman below the wrist.
14	WACKY:	Perry is a colorful young man with a flair for lace
15		cuffs and Silly Putty wrist watches.
16	WIFFY:	Received national recognition when he led a march
17		of followers into Central Park, forming them into a spit
18		curl formation and directing them as they teased three
19		elm trees to death.
20	WACKY:	Perry hasn't changed his undershirt in three
21		months, thereby eliminating the need for deodorant
22		which might pollute the atmosphere.
23	WIFFY:	Perry's trademark: the beard that covers most of his
24		sensitive face was grown because he wanted to look like
25		his mother.
26	WACKY:	His group, the Leaping Leotards, wants clean air,
27		edible drinking water and the right to sing the blues.
28	WIFFY:	*(Holding up picture)* Glomb Fleden.
29	WACKY:	Heir to the famous Fleden Reducing Salon fortune,
30		Glomb has been living off the fat of the land for many
31		years.
32	WIFFY:	Fiery Glomb heads the forceful East Wing
33		Autocrats.
34	WACKY:	The group has been charged with defacing the
35		posters of six federal judges.

1 WIFFY: And . . . three *real* federal judges.
2 WACKY: Glomb has written forceful and incisive editorials
3   upholding the right to picket fences, the necessity of
4   weaning beavers in distress and the establishment of a
5   grievance committee for shorter-than-average rich people.
6 WIFFY: An idealist, Glomb's editorials have often been
7   reprinted — in his own magazine — The Glitz Group.
8 WACKY: A congenial fellow when relaxed, Glomb likes to
9   drink oolong tea, and bowl with mutants.
10 WIFFY: Good luck out there, and happy protesting.
11 WIFFY and WACKY: This has been a public service
12   announcement.
13 .
14
15
16
17
18
19
20
21
22
23
24
25
26
27
28
29
30
31
32
33
34
35

#50

A Visit to Washington, D.C. — A Capitol Idea

CAST: ANNOUNCER, male or female, On-Stage or Off; ANN/DAN Pennings, hostess/host of a local TV program. Anywhere from thirty to forty, and is quietly confident in her/his job; PAM/SAM Greeley, a high school senior who is being interviewed about her/his recent trip to the nation's capitol.

SETTING: Interview set-up with table or desk, two chairs and simulated mike. PAM/SAM holds notes of the diary she/he kept of her/his visit. She/he will read from the notes.

ANNOUNCER: **Many thousands of people visit Washington, D.C. and surrounding areas. And rightly so. Everyone should walk around in this historic city, the home of George Washington, Thomas Jefferson and several assorted senators and representatives who shall remain nameless. But we all know who they are. All visitors do. Or will.**

    One recent visitor to Washington was Pam Greeley, a senior at *(Any local name of school)* **High School. Here she is about to tell Ann Pennings of WWWW-TV about the trip.** *(OPENING: Both performers are seated. NOTE: Use names applying to gender chosen to perform.)*

ANN: **Welcome back, Pam. Enjoy your trip to the capitol?**

PAM: *(Smiling)* **Very interesting time. I kept a diary of my visit.**

ANN: **I'm sure our viewers will be very interested, Pam. You got the ball.** *(Pointing to PAM)*

PAM: **Thank you. I must tell you some of the names were changed because I don't have congressional immunity.**

ANN: *(Chuckles)* **Right.**

PAM: **9 a.m. — Awake in luxury hotel, dress in lavish suite, walk down to velvet carpeted lobby, down flower covered**

1	walk— elude roving band of muggers, hop into bullet-
2	proofed taxicab and speed to Capitol Hill.

ANN: A rousing start indeed.

PAM: 9:15 — Session gets underway as chaplain prays for senators. Chaplain looks closely at senators and prays for the rest of the country.

9:30 — Head of senatorial junket about to take off for ten-day trip to Paris points out group will be saving taxpayer's money — they won't be taking their wives along.

10 a.m. — Recess, as cleaning lady comes in to vacuum Senator Todd's hair.

10:45 — Russian embassy sends note of protest saying Washington police harassed the embassy this morning and have towed away an illegally parked tank.

And then I moved to a few committee hearings. This is where much of the real work gets done.

ANN: Right. The nuts and bolts, meat and potatoes of government.

PAM: Exactly. 11 a.m. — House committee investigates alleged racism in certain area of country. Congressman from that area denies racism, saying, "If I'm lying may the good Lord above strike me down."

11:15 — Services for congressman.

11:30 — Over to House Appropriations Committee where American Civil Liberties Rehabilitation Group asks for funds to charter bus for mass prison break.

11:45 — Secretary of Labor testifies at hearing that it takes Russian citizen three hours of work for money to buy a pound of butter, while it takes an American only twenty-two minutes. The secretary's question: "Where do we find an American today willing to *work* twenty-two minutes?"

12 noon — Talk of labor tires out congressmen and they retire to their offices for Rest and Rehabilitation.

1	12:30 — Relaxation time as twenty senators
2	swimming nude in the capitol pool have a fifty-yard race.
3	Senator Margaret Glendenning comes in first.
4	1 p.m. — Senate committee takes up issue of stopping
5	crime on Washington streets. Police chief suggests
6	moving those streets to Delaware.
7	1:30 — American Equal Rights Committee convinces
8	congressional committee it is old-fashioned and
9	discriminatory against hiring women.
10	1:40 — Woman hired as Senate men's room attendant.
11	2 p.m. — Stand outside closed hearing room and
12	eavesdrop as senators grill Secretary of State.
13	2:15 — Secretary of States flees to Virginia seeking
14	political asylum.
15	2:30 — Kentucky senator announces the latest
16	Student Exchange Scholarship has been awarded to Jim
17	Clorid, Kenosha, Wisconsin's village idiot. *(Any area city*
18	*can be used.)*
19	3 p.m. — Senator Mike Garley says country is
20	perfectly safe from enemy attack.
21	3:05 — Senator Garley arrested by police for speeding
22	to his fall-out shelter in Maryland.
23	3:30 — Eavesdrop on secret CIA hearing on more
24	funds for combatting Communism. Four experts voted
25	this way — affirmative, affirmative, affirmative and nyet.
26	ANN: More eavesdropping. You certainly gave your ears a
27	good workout.
28	PAM: Public's right to know, eh?
29	ANN: Exactly. Continue, Pam.
30	PAM: 4:30 — Let-up time to relax. Lotta Boomer, in honor of
31	"See America First Promotion Day," shows up to accept
32	plaque wearing dress made of map of USA.
33	4:35 — New Hampshire delegation files formal protest,
34	complaining of New Hampshire's location on dress.
35	4:36 — Fiery New Hampshirite tries to rearrange map.

1		4:37 — Lotta Boomer runs screaming from Congress,
2		chased by New Hampshire delegation.
3		5 p.m. — New Hampshire delegation returns. Requests
4		today be named "See Lotta Boomer First Day."
5	ANN:	Statehood loyalty. Noble, very noble.
6	PAM:	Right. 5:30 — Back to work. Senate Finance Committee
7		reports too many Secret Service men are on government
8		payroll. Reveal that six of them are still guarding Coolidge.
9		Dinner break.
10		8 p.m. — Attend lavish cocktail party attended by
11		many top government officials. Secretary of State admits
12		these are tough times, but denies he bought a used
13		Kamikaze plane.
14		8:15 — President says he will attend Protestant,
15		Catholic and Jewish services this weekend, being
16		perfectly impartial. He will bestow equal blessings on all
17		clergymen.
18		8:30 — Beautiful Betsy Klinger, former Miss Texas,
19		says she has political ambitions. Congressmen gather
20		around to see if she will throw her blouse into the ring.
21		9 p.m. — Washington officially closes down. Armored
22		trucks transport guests on winding, unannounced route
23		to get them home safely through crime-ridden streets.
24		9:30 — Watch from luxury hotel's iron-barred windows
25		as police and construction workers silently begin moving
26		Washington's streets to Delaware.
27	ANN:	Thanks, Pam. I see you made it home all right. How did
28		you return? Any problems?
29	PAM:	No trouble at all. That underground tunnel from
30		Washington to *(Local city)* is perfectly safe.
31		
32		
33		
34		
35		

ABOUT THE AUTHOR
BILL MAJESKI

Bill Majeski has had four plays which enjoyed successful runs at the small dinner theater level — Little Lake Dinner Theater in Canonsburg, Pennsylvania, and the Playhouse Dinner Theater in Amesbury, Massachusetts.

Two of his one-acts ran for two weeks at the off-off-Broadway Quaigh Theater in New York City.

Twenty-four of his plays — all comedies — have been published by leading publishers of dramatic works. These are presented throughout the country chiefly by high school, college and community theater groups.

He was a staff writer on the Johnny Carson Tonight Show and has written material for Bob Newhart, Steve Allen, Phyllis Diller, Ed McMahon and others.

He has written four nonfiction books of humor and information for several major publishers.

Many of his humor pieces have appeared in newspapers including the New York Times, the Los Angeles Times, New York News and many more. He has written articles for magazines ranging from Playboy to the Saturday Review.

ORDER FORM

MERIWETHER PUBLISHING LTD.
P.O. BOX 7710
COLORADO SPRINGS, CO 80933
TELEPHONE: (719) 594-4422

Please send me the following books:

_____**Doubletalk — Comedy Duets for Actors #TT-B186 $9.95**
by Bill Majeski
A collection of comedy duets for actors

_____**On Stage! Short Plays for Acting**
Students #TT-B165   **$9.95**
by Robert Mauro
24 short one-act plays for acting practice

_____**TV Scenes for Actors #TT-B137**   **$14.95**
by Sigmund A. Stoler
Selected short scenes from the Golden Age of TV Drama

_____**Winning Monologs for Young Actors #TT-B127 $7.95**
by Peg Kehret
Honest-to-life monologs for young actors

_____**Two Character Plays for Student Actors #TT-B174 $7.95**
by Robert Mauro
A collection of 15 one-act plays

_____**Original Audition Scenes for Actors #TT-B129 $9.95**
by Garry Michael Kluger
A book of professional-level dialogs and monologs

_____**57 Original Auditions for Actors #TT-B181**   **$6.95**
by Eddie Lawrence
A workbook of monologs for actors

I understand that I may return any book
for a full refund if not satisfied.

NAME: _____

ORGANIZATION NAME: _____

ADDRESS: _____

CITY: _____ STATE: _____ ZIP: _____

PHONE: _____

☐ **Check Enclosed**
☐ **Visa or Master Card #**_____

Signature: _____

(required for Visa/Mastercard orders)

COLORADO RESIDENTS: Please add 3% sales tax.
SHIPPING: Include $1.50 for the first book and 50¢ for each additional book ordered.

☐ *Please send me a copy of your complete catalog of books or plays.*